D0432278

THERE'LL ALWAYS
∽ BE AN ∽
ENGLAND

THERE'LL ALWAYS
~ BE AN ~
ENGLAND

Social Stereotypes from the *Telegraph*

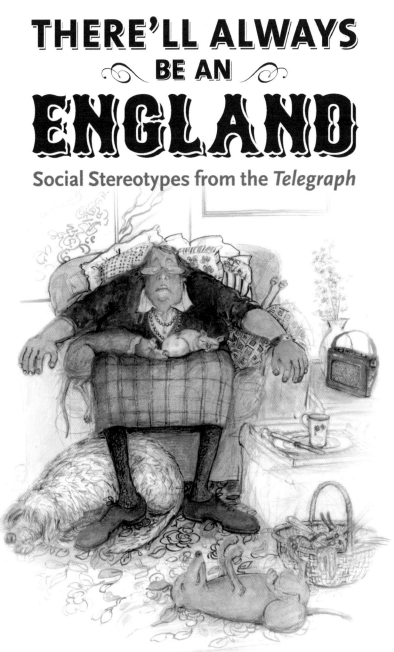

Victoria Mather and Sue Macartney-Snape

Constable · London

Constable & Robinson Ltd
3 The Lanchesters
162 Fulham Palace Road
London W6 9ER
www.constablerobinson.com

First published in the UK by Constable,
an imprint of Constable & Robinson Ltd, 2010

Copyright © Victoria Mather, Sue Macartney-Snape and Telegraph
Group Limited, 2010

Designed by Smith & Gilmour, London

The rights of Victoria Mather and Sue Macartney-Snape to be
identified as the authors of this work have been asserted by them
in accordance with the Copyright, Designs and Patents Act 1988

All rights reserved. This book is sold subject to the condition that it
shall not, by way of trade or otherwise, be lent, re-sold, hired out or
otherwise circulated in any form of binding or cover other than that
in which it is published and without a similar condition including
this condition being imposed on the subsequent purchaser.

A copy of the British Library Cataloguing in
Publication data is available from the British Library

ISBN: 978-1-84901-557-8

Printed and bound in China by C&C Offset Printing Co.,Ltd

1 3 5 7 9 10 8 6 4 2

Contents

For Max Hastings, with affection

Nine Hundred Social Stereotypes is a cause of celebration, a miracle of longevity in newspaper columns of which *There'll Always be an England* is the tenth anthology. Back in 1993, the prototype of Stereotypes was a twinkle in the eye of Max Hastings, then editor of the *Daily Telegraph*. Sue and I made our debut at the Chelsea Flower Show in his special edition, gently satirizing the characters amongst the chrysanthemums. It seemed like a good idea at the time and sprang into being fully formed in Emma Soames's *Telegraph Magazine*. The following seventeen years have been a social rollercoaster; a plethora of new stereotypes have constantly emerged from the shadows of new technology, New Labour and new social mores. Yet the column has remained consistently loyal to the English way of life, which paddles bravely against the current. Despite the ubiquity of email, Facebook, mobiles, political correctitude, WAGs and low-cost airlines – none of which existed, or only in nascent form, in 1993 – our hearts are still in Decorating the Church, the Pub Quiz and the damp British Holiday.

Myriad thanks are due to Michelle Lavery, editor of the *Telegraph Magazine*, for continuing to espouse Social Stereotypes with such enthusiasm. Also at the *Telegraph* we are indebted to Paul Davies, who edits the column with patient guidance; Denis Piggott, Jeremy Farr and Sophie de Rosée (née Robinson) – inspiration for The Bridezilla (I am sure she wasn't one really). Other Stereotypes moles include Lucy Blyth, Georgia Coleridge, Ewa Lewis, and Lesley-Jane Nicholson. Peter Andreae inspired the stoically sock-wearing Englishman Abroad; the Diffident Veteran is dedicated to Camilla Osborne, a soul of patriotism. She never forgets that there would not be an England if it were not for our brave, splendid Armed Forces past and present.

We owe the publication of this book, together with its predecessors, to the wisdom and kindness of our publishing guru Caroline Knox. Andreas Campomar nobly championed our cause at Constable & Robinson.

Victoria Mather
London 2010

A Stereotypical Foreword
by Sandi Toksvig

I am delighted to be here fulfilling what I see as a social stereotype of a slightly bemused foreigner, introducing two very nice women whose view of the world seems so quintessentially English. Born in Denmark and raised in the United States, I nevertheless visited England often. I remember it as a curious place of one-bar electric fires fighting draughts that whistled across rooms where we sat trying to break trays of toffee with a small metal hammer, while the wireless told us the weather in somewhere called German Bight. What was clear from my English relatives was that they represented the redoubtable qualities of an unvanquishable island race. The stories of their suburban heroics in World War Two – 'Every house in the street was bombed by Mr Hitler except ours because Granny wouldn't allow it' – made it very clear that 'There'll Always be an England'.

I have now resided in the UK for just over three decades and although I still have an outside eye I like to think I can now recognize these social stereotypes. I spent some years in a small English village, where I was on nodding acquaintance with at least one unmarried *Lady Cyclist* whose way with a root vegetable was the envy of the parish and where you wouldn't have been the least bit surprised to discover that the vicar had twinned the church 'with a mud hut evangelical worship centre in the Congo'. I have lived alongside the *Lawn Fetishist* whose devotion to the scarification of his patch verged on the worrying and I have stayed with people who believed central heating to be a luxury item. I have sat at Glyndebourne next to some poor fellow whose loathing of opera was sadly outweighed by the social need to attend weddings where the bridegroom seemed a 'forgotten accessory'.

I think that I know these people, that I have met and observed them; but I am also clear that I could not have pinned them down the way Victoria and Sue have managed. For that, I'm afraid, you do need to be English. In this instance I am merely the visitor who can only stand back and admire.

Enjoy.

The Afternoon Snooze

HERMIONE AND THE dogs were up at six, patrolling the garden, a swift bit of rabbiting in the wood, feeding the chickens, checking Mr Fox hadn't had his wicked way. Then porridge on the Aga (Hermione) and a nice chopped lamb's heart (dogs) that's stewed all night in the top left oven. 'Good for your tummies, chaps. Now don't you go pushing all the bikkie to one side.' A bit of John Humphrys to make them all cross enough to tackle the day and then off to the village for the newspaper, coley for the cat and a companionable chat with the butcher while he's boning and mincing a shoulder of lamb for Hermione's shepherd's pie. 'Another bridge evening, Miss Bracegirdle? You spoil your guests, you do. Lady Gusset – although, mind you, I shouldn't say this – only buys the cheapest cuts. Now, how about some pig's ears for the doggies?' Hermione, quietly triumphant that Phyllis Gusset's food is so inferior, progresses to the farm shop and splashes out on the new season's brussels sprouts.

Returning home, she disagrees vehemently with Jenni Murray on *Woman's Hour*, peels potatoes, makes the shepherd's pie (ready for bottom right oven at five), whips up an apple snow, deadheads the last roses and removes the wisteria leaves from the gutter. Then she and the dogs, exhausted with barking anxiously at the bottom of her ladder, retire for lunch. Soup and toast (Hermione), pig's ears (dogs). None of them makes it through *The Archers* (who can, since it has become a dirge about dementia?) before they are asleep, perchance to dream – of Scotland and salmon (Hermione), of ratsy-patsies (dogs), of goldfish (the cat). A contented purry-snoring reverberates. The Italian greyhound serves as a hot-water bottle on Hermione's lap. The Roberts radio burbles and there's a comforting aroma of wet dog and venerable tweed. The wood-burning stove soothes the somnolent masses, the snooze of the just who've slaved all morning. At four there'll be various snorts and harrumphs and a 'Goodness, is that the time?'

The Crashing Bore

HARRY HARUMPH IS your man if you need to know how to get to Scotland avoiding the M1 by using the M40, crossing over on the M69, joining the brute at Leicester Forest East, then getting orf as soon as damn possible using the M18 to join the good old Great North Road at Doncaster. Mind you, there's a shocking roadwork near the A64 and don'tchaknow that nine people have been killed on the A9 north of Perth this season?

Grist to the relentless grind of Harry's mill are roadworks, the iniquity of speed cameras and foolishness of satnav: 'Our son gave me one. Put in Chatsworth and you end up in the Clover Nook industrial estate.'

How Harry got to Glensporran, including every traffic cone, lasts the entire first course, during which Lady Violet thinks about her rose order at David Austin (is the Paul's Himalayan Musk really a good idea?). She tried, 'Tell me, Colonel Harumph, as I know you were in Kenya. What do you think about the current political situation?' but Harry was negotiating the mess caused by installing trams in Edinburgh: 'The Scottish parliament has more money than sense.'

Round two, over the string-dry roast venison, is about recycling, the shock waves of which are reverberating about Chipping on the Wold. 'We've a black box for bottles, and a green box for newspapers, and a pink box with purple spots for kitchen waste – thing's a bloody nightmare. Marigold doesn't know her compost from her cardboard. The old girl's in a terrible state, all to save a polar bear.'

As Harry picks meat out of his teeth and progresses from recycling to immigration – 'Ridiculous – we should hang a sign saying "Full Up" on UK PLC' – Lady Violet wonders whether Arthur has recorded *Foyle's War*. By the raspberries Harry is on to fuel prices, all the fault of the Russkies, and the loony leftism of the BBC, speaking straight ahead into a void of mahogany and silver sticks. Lady Violet is wondering whether she switched on her electric blanket, when Col. Harumph snaps to. 'Keen-yah, didya say? Now I can tell you a thing or two ...' She wishes she hadn't asked.

The Toy Infestation

JONAH LOVES HIS wooden spoon – bang, bang, bang. The fire engine, the pirate ship, the wonky castle (put together by Daddy) are transient pleasures compared to 'My wdn poon'. If his mother, Evie, wasn't too exhausted to think, she'd wonder why she spent good money on the ignored toys that have transformed her sitting room into a Hades of Hamleys.

The wrapping always seems more successful than the presents. Ribbon gives hours of pleasure strangling poor Teddy; cardboard and paper are such fun if set alight. Evie learnt to hide matches as soon as Jonah hit eighteen months. Evie's mother says children are hopelessly spoilt These Days and when Evie was a child she was allowed one dolly and That Was That. Didn't Evie read in the *Guardian* that there are sixty-two pieces of Lego for everyone on the planet? 'Although most of them seem to be on your carpet, dear.' Sniff. That grandmotherly sniff of disapproval, harbinger of the lecture on how childcare isn't what it used to be in Her Day.

'Surely some Slovenian immigrant would be grateful to be a home help. Not the same as darling old Nanny, of course, but she might help you tidy up. Evie? Do listen, dear. Look at this mess. Where am I supposed to sit? I have rheumatism, you know.' Evie has been looking at the mess for post-baby eternity and no longer notices it. She imagines it's why so many thirtysomething parents eat in Pizza Express: can't be fished to tidy up, too poor for the posh Italian.

Jonah is about to throw himself off the table. Good luck to him. Evie doesn't remember Noah being so hyperactive, but she doesn't remember much any more. Noah lives his toy life behind the sofa – a no-go area of dust and plastic farm animals – away from Jonah's full-on vandalism. On Saturday morning there is the ghastly scream, the exquisite pain of a stressed-out barefoot banker father stepping on a piece of Lego.

The Comical Dog Show

DIGGER IS MORTIFIED to be dressed up in a straw hat with paper flowers made by Mother in arts and crafts. He feels like a package tourist. Not that he has ever been a package tourist, being deficient in the Pet Passport department, but he saw them when Mother took him to Gatwick Airport to meet Marcus on his return from his Spanish exchange. Hordes of lobster-pink wobbly people with sombreros, many carrying stuffed donkeys.

Marcus has explained to Digger that they have to do the Hat Contest in the Parish Comical Dog Show for charity. The vicar has twinned St Botolph's with a mud hut evangelical worship centre in the Congo. Digger has explained this to Horace, who is dressed in a fez that his master, Ned, disinterred from the dressing-up box. Muffin is doing her Patience on a Monument imitation, having been kitted out with fairy wings and a halo by Marina. Marina keeps saying, 'Isn't this all such fun?', which is a sad reflection on the fact that anthropomorphism benefits humans rather than animals.

Wilbur, a furious Norwich terrier in a top hat, is well aware of this and, devoted to his mistress, Posy, as he is, has vicious plans for the verger's ankles. Not to mention the lady curate with the Vicar of Dibley haircut. 'Who's a jolly doggie, then?' Snarl, snap, bite. Posy is in tears but Colonel Truscott mops her up and says, 'Well done, Wilbur. Just how I feel about women priests. Smashing little chap, you've got there, Posy. Let's arrange a marriage with my Violet. Pups, eh? Now, that's what I call fun. Now let's all find an ice-cream. What flavour do you like, Wilbur? King James' Bible or Happy-Clappy? Splendid, splendid – such a good idea to put chocolate chips in the KJ Bible.' Wilbur having been given an ASBO, the others trudge round the judging ring. Horace has to be dragged. Digger digs in under Marcus's feet. Muffin and Marina look sweet and shy. The vicar, mindful of whose mummy and daddy gave most to the church bells appeal, is delighted to award them the first rosette. 'Dear little Muffin. How are your wonderful parents, Marina?'

'Divorcing, Vicar. Sorree, Muffin has peed on your cassock.'

The Diffident Veteran

BINGO JACKSON HAS arthritic knees and a dodgy hip, mere inconveniences that would never prevent him from getting up when a lady enters the room. 'My dear girl, I'm having a little whikky. What about a G&T? Lots of G and less T. I've finished the crossword and Bader's demanding to go outies. Aren't you, Bader? Furry fellow, would make an excellent gun cleaner. Pop him out the back door, dear girl, while I build you a tincture.' All ladies, regardless of age, are dear girls. His niece, Camilla, is a favourite – always brings a spiffing fish pie. When little, she called him Uncle Air-Commo; now she gently winkles his war stories out of him. 'Uncle A-C, WingCo, DFC, over and out, I don't want to read about what you did in your obituary in the *Daily Telegraph*.' So Bingo is teased into memories.

'We were told to support the Russkies advancing from the east in 1945. Bloody awful winter. Our Lancaster was coned by searchlights and I had to do corkscrews to puzzle the anti-aircraft chappies. Talking of corkscrews – white wine?' Over the fish pie he confides to this particular dear girl that he did a bit in Calcutta.

'The Red Road, sort of Piccadilly thingy, was turned into a fighter runway. Marvellous. One could eat at Firpo's, quite the best restaurant in town, and take off within four minutes.' Camilla drives him and Bader to visit infirm comrades – 'The RAF family, we're all a bit doddery now' – and hears conversational wisps from hospice armchairs of that first time over Hamburg that Bingo and Charlie saw a Messerschmitt 262 jet fighter.

'Luckily the Huns didn't build enough of those to have a real go at us.' He's written her a letter saying, 'I'm sorry I didn't tell you about Dresden. I flew eleven hours that night, briefed to go for the marshalling yards. Couldn't bear to talk about it, dearest girl. God bless.' She'll read in the obituary that 'John Jackson, a pilot with an aim so accurate he was known as Bingo, displayed a complete lack of self-importance and was much loved and admired by all ranks.' She knew that already.

The Lunch Companions

MARJORIE AND NEIL lunch once a month. He is widowed and she is divorced. Her husband Brian left her for his secretary, and the residual bitterness for this lack of imagination shows in the tight delta of lines round her mouth.

Neil and Marjorie – she was his wife's best friend – like an old-fashioned restaurant, or Neil's club. 'The best restaurant is the restaurant that knows you best,' Neil says, and they have to have a restaurant with a carpet, not new-fangled floorboards, otherwise they can't hear each other. It's difficult enough when short-term memory loss strikes after the claret and Neil can't remember what Marjorie's name is. 'Used to be Daphne's partner for Ladies' Wednesday Bridge Afternoons,' he has to think to himself, moving slightly sideways as if to seek the waiter. Neil likes to know the names of the waiters, too; it is a comfortable little sophistication of the sort he finds reassuring.

The trouble is that in a changing world he's finding Romanian nomenclature tricky. Marjorie is happy to be called Madam, an echo from the happy staff-greased years she spent with Brian when he was posted to Hong Kong. Before handover, of course. What on earth did Mrs Thatcher think she was doing? Wonderful woman in all other ways but handed a British earthly paradise back to commies. Neil and Maisie, Marjorie and Brian met racing at Happy Valley. They remember it well during the first course. Children the same age, apartments in Mid-Levels, drinks in the Captain's Bar at the Mandarin. 'Wonder what it's like now?' muses Marjorie.

'Only place you can smoke indoors, special licence thingy, damned smart,' harrumphs Neil, proud of insider knowledge obtained at the nineteenth hole from Snorter Garrett.

The statutory round-up of the children – Charlie in IT, which neither understands, and Susannah with her second baby – gets them to cheese and pudding.

'Same time next month, old girl?'

'Thank you, Neil. It would be lovely.' They depart by bus to their individual cells of loneliness.

The Bridezilla

Sophie is in the me-zone. 'It's my day, it's my wedding, it's my party, I'll cry if I want to. Mummy, did you remember that tissues have to be put in all the front pews in case the bridesmaids puke?'

Mummy, staring up in horror at this monster she's spawned, says meekly, 'Yes, Sophie, of course, Sophie.' Where is the dear little Sophiewophie-puffly-pot of the toddler years? The sweet Sophie who loved bunny-wunnies? The eager-to-please Sophie who was so nice to children and old people? The vulnerable Sophie who was a homebird in the teenage years while the Jakes and Gemmas were vomiting cider? She's transmogrified into tantrum Sophie. Her wedding is the most important day in everyone's life. How dare the Smutton-Muttons be on holiday in Venice? How could Emily be going to her brother's twenty-first? What is it with Rebecca that she's having her wedding on the same day? Can you bee-leeeeve it? The bridegroom, an often forgotten accessory, is deployed on defuse. 'Say, Sophs, it's all cool. Chill, girl.' At which point *Bridezilla* bursts into tears, says he doesn't understand, and huddles into her mobile, sobbing to her mother about whether to have bows or knots on the ribbon around the napkins at the wedding dinner. The vision of loveliness in her Sassi Holford dress, Aunt Laetitia's tiara and godmother Juliet's veil has been on intravenous Rescue Remedy for weeks.

Last night she had a dream that the dress hadn't arrived and she had to walk down the aisle in orange plus-fours. The make-up artist dropped out – 'Mummy,' sob, 'who could be more important than me?'

Harvey the hairdresser is her only centre of calm in the storm. Harvey knows how to deal with a tiara and bridesmaids eating their lily-of-the-valley head-dresses. Sophie's father is on his knees, praying all this may pass. One day his Sophie will be back, little duckie, possibly with a little duckling in her arms. He longs to be Grandpa, but currently he feels ground under her Manolo heel. 'How much did those cost?'

'But Daddy, this is my day.' Sophie's brothers, both ushers, say, 'Gosh, sis, you've got a zit and you're sooo BZ.' Sophie trickles tears: 'Stop calling me Bridezilla, you beasts.'

The Uncontrollable Gundog

JEEVES IS HAVING a lovely time.

Pop-bang! Wheeee! Thump!

Another pheasant hits the ground. 'I must go and fetch it for Master,' and he runs in merrily to pinch Sir Nately Scures's bird, a spectacular high shot that prompted murmurs of 'Well done', particularly from Julia Climber, who knows Sir Nately is one of the best shots in the country and would like to be asked to shoot at Scures. Meanwhile, Roderick Twitton-Whitton, Jeeves' master, is blowing desperately on his dog whistle saying, 'Sorry, Nately, sorry, everyone. Sort it out after the drive. Jeeves, whatho! Come here, you damned dog.' Jeeves doesn't want to come here, it's all much too exciting.

If pinioned to the ground by his master's peg with a metal corkscrew he whines piteously. Sir Nately says, 'Roderick, do something about that dog of yours. I can hear its squeaking through my ear defenders. Bloody annoying.' On the way to the next drive, bump-bump-bump on straw bales in the trailer, Jeeves crawls over everyone's knees, leaving wet mud all over Julia's suede trousers. 'Oh, I say, so sorry. He's only young, I'm afraid.' Roderick proffers Julia a spotted red hankie and offers dry cleaning. 'I doubt even Jeeves could repair the damage Jeeves has done,' Julia says tartly. The dog puts his head on her knee to do the melting, chocolate-eyed, I'm-really-awfully-sweet act. Doesn't wash. 'Why on earth haven't you sent him to gundog school with a keeper, Roderick?' Roderick says he's tried that. 'Didn't seem to have the desired effect. Think the poor chap was homesick.' Sir Nately and Julia roll their eyes as one. Sir Nately barks that spaniels are an absolute menace. 'Now you take Purdey here, proper Lab, never moves off my peg. Stern discipline. Lives in a kennel. I bet you have that hooligan tucked up by the Aga.' Next Roderick tries to anchor Jeeves by tying his cartridge case round the dog's neck, unfortunately forgetting to close it so that when Jeeves does another joyous dash some 200 cartridges are spread across Partridge Bottom. At lunch, just as his master is tucking into the restorative claret, Jeeves picks a blood-curdling fight with Purdey. Roderick will certainly never be asked to shoot at Scures.

The County Magistrate

BARBARA HAS BEEN the Boadicea of the Bench for twenty-five years. Up with nonsense she will not put. Once, cases in Bury St Vole (where they did indeed bury St Vole in the 13th century) were proper ones about poaching and burglary. Now Barbara's valuable time away from the herbaceous border is wasted by wheelie-bin desperados and speeding offenders. 'Mr Hopbottom, could you try a little harder than claiming that you didn't think the speed limit applied after midnight?'

Nor is Barbara having any truck with the fellow who claimed he was a tropical fish specialist and it was clearly the weight of the water in his fish tanks that propelled his white van at 80 mph down Highwayman Hill. Nor is 'I collided with a stationary truck coming the other way' very convincing. There have been defendants turned into pillars of salt when Barbara, pearls gleaming white and perm iron-grey, has leant forward, tapping her pencil, full of interest in their stuttering attempts to claim that 'The guy was all over the road. I had to swerve a number of times before I hit him.'

Barbara regards it as her moral duty to be a magistrate. In the happy days when Arthur Tideswell was caught in the glare of police headlights on Lord Connaught's estate, saying 'Gedoff, gedoff!' to a deer wrapped around his shoulders, Barbara had adjourned.

Returning to court, she had announced the case dismissed and said in a stage whisper, 'Tip from me for the future, young man: don't do it again.'

Now she's dealing with PC fools and charlatans. The other day the Crown Prosecution Service lawyer asked the defendant, 'Could either driver have done anything to avoid the accident?' And the defendant answered, 'Travelled by bus, sir?'

Barbara gives all concerned a good wigging. The clerk is given Barbara's clutched-pearl position, hand-to-throat, with stentorian strictures about inconsequential cases regarding rubbish-collecting facilities and idiotic binge drinking.

'Miss Pantsdown, are you really telling me that your car left the road and you were later found in a ditch by some stray cows?'

The Wannabe Wag

ABBIE HAS SOME difficulty remembering which parts of her are real and which are enhanced – the fake nails (hand and toe), the eyelashes (but they're made of real hair), the clip-in hair extensions (ditto, so they were real). The pneumatic embonpoint was a present from her mam for her twenty-first. 'Well, love, if you really, really want it. You don't look a bit flat-chested to me but all I want is for you to be happy.' So, best front forward, Abbie moved from South Shields to a terraced semi in Heaton, Newcastle, to follow her dream of becoming a Geordie It Girl and marrying a footballer. Mind you, Ashley's put her off a bit. Bastard, what with Cheryl being so lovely – 'spect he was jealous of her success, the moron. Abbie, who gets her intellectual stimulation through Facebook, can quite understand why her virtual friend Sharon shared the info that 34 per cent of women would swap their man for Cheryl Cole's wardrobe. Shar got it from MyCelebrityFashion.co.uk but Abbie's mam said how did anyone know that Cheryl's clothes would fit. 'She's a walking hairpin, that one. Now, love, are you eating properly? Come home and have a nice roast.'

Abbie lives on beansprouts and steamed chicken and works at Beauty 4 All in 'toon' when she's not doing spinning classes at the David Lloyd sports centre in Jesmond. The Newcastle Falcons train there and Abbie puts on a pout and a wiggle whenever she saunters through the juice bar. The membership's crippling but worth it for the fit guys. On Monday she starts planning for Saturday night, buying her outfit on ASOS.com, a copy of the latest Cheryl or Kate Moss at a snip or, if flush, going to All Saints in Fenwick for a blow-out on a bit of coo-tour. She and her girlfriends start getting ready at 4 p.m. – smoky eyes, plumpy nude lips, caramel legs courtesy of three sessions at the Electric Beach. They drink vodka to get in the mood and totter out on vertiginous gladiator heels, with titchy white fake Birkins to carry lipstick, mascara, condoms, credit card and taxi money to Tup Tup Palace, the China White of the North. Abbie shimmies by the VIP area where the footballers sit. If invited in she'll feel all celeby, drink champagne and float home coatless despite the biting wind.

The Christmas Stocking

JOSIE HAS SPENT all year collecting amusing little nothings for the stockings of her husband, children, Granny, the divorced girlfriend who's coming to stay, widowed Uncle Fergus who's staying rather too long, Godmother Isabel and the dog. Nothings that actually amount to several hundred pounds, and many of which she has mislaid by putting them in a safe place. She started out heroically in the January sales, hunter-gathering discounted boxes of Floris soap for Granny and Godmother. They must be somewhere. Then there was the trip to Morocco when she bought belts in the leather souk which, when stored in the spare-room wardrobe, smelt of dead goat. The beadwork bibelots – purses, necklaces, adorable evening bags – made in townships in Cape Town mysteriously incurred £150 in overweight on the return journey. Josie thinks trying to save money is very unrewarding.

There was a magic moment when she found last year's stocking fillers, bought at Abigail Purseglove's Christmas Fayre, in the airing cupboard. Yay! There was a heady I'm-dreaming-of-a-free-Christmas moment until she realized all the hand cream had solidified. There has been mail-order frenzy, getting bridge cards with Uncle Fergus' initials and thrashing the Lakeland catalogue for mini-jams, crystallized ginger and tins of chocolate mice. Will the Greedy Pig Fridge Alert, a fridge magnet that goes oink-oink if anyone raids the leftovers, give her daughter anorexia? Too late now. Maybe it'll stop the divorcee savaging the white wine. Josie has now fallen back on the hardy annuals of olive oil, coffee and tennis balls for her husband because he says, 'Darling, you really can only go on doing stockings if they're practical.' Which is what men say.

Josie loves doing stockings, the lumpy promise, the crackle of the wrapping, the little special pressies hidden among the Tesco Squeezy Orange Blossom Honey: a pretty brooch for Granny, a disc for Godmother Isabel's charm bracelet with her dog's name engraved on it. Books and scented candles are laden into Josie's cut-up fishnet tights. Such a saving on buying stockings.

The Magic Skip

CORDELIA AND GEOFFREY are downsizing. The oil bill at the Old Rectory is extortionate and the children have left home, one fortunately being an estate agent. He off-loaded the Old Rec and now Cordelia and Geoffrey are are throwing their lives' detritus into the skip.

Ah, the skip! Nothing, other than *Bleak House* and *Inspector Morse* on the telly, has given them such pleasure for yonks. Gone is all the old chutney circa 1995; gone are the quilted bedheads inherited from Geoffrey's mother; gone is the furniture acquired in the age of faux-bamboo fashionability. How hideous was that?

They feel marvellously chipper at this catharsis. Cordelia has drawn the line at throwing away the *Tatlers* from the year she came out – 'Oh, look, there's Tessa Hurly-Burly. Wasn't she ravishing? I saw her the other day in Peter Jones and she's got more lines than Clapham Junction' – but Geoffrey has had a chucking orgy of old water bills and his father's bank statements written in sloping script, with letters signed 'I Remain, Sir, Yours Respectfully'. Fat chance of the National Westminster being so oleaginous.

Consigning her mother-in-law's hideous standard lamps to the skip, complete with revolting fringed lampshades, has liberated Cordelia into a new woman. Plus the clear-out of Shopping Mistakes: the pottery vase bought in Crete on honeymoon that looked so charming in Elounda never quite translated to Nottinghamshire.

As odd glasses with chips in the rim, ghastly mugs and aberrant plates arc their way into oblivion, Cordelia and Geoffrey have found nothing is so satisfactory as the sound of breaking glass and china. The trashing of their past is licensed delinquency.

There was a terrible moment at 10 p.m. when, after several celebratory whiskies, Geoffrey decided to retrieve his old train set and was bottoms-up in the skip for hours, but otherwise they have been superbly ruthless.

Cordelia finally chucked her wedding dress. She wonders if someone sorting their rubbish in China will find it.

The Unpublished Author

DAMIAN IS DANGEROUSLY near to writing the first sentence of his novel, but just before taking the plunge he thought he'd nip to the Procrastinators' Club for an inspirational glass or three. 'Your finest house claret, Isidore; the Muse is upon me!' Barmen at the Procrastinators' are always called Isidore, regardless of the fact that the current incumbent is Romanian. It suits him rather better than the previous cheeky chappie from Essex, a fact that Damian – 'I am absurdly perceptive' – has vaguely noted for detail in chapter three when his hero surfaces from a maelstrom of drink and drugs, lying on a carpet patterned with vomit in a club not unlike the PC. Damian is not writing a romantic novel. Marian Keyes and Sophie Kinsella shouldn't be shaking in their shoes that so often adorn the covers of their oeuvre in airports. Damian's account of the torture of growing up in Notting Hill, the parental abuse of being sent to Eton, the misery of partying at Oxford, the descent into addiction and despair, is unlikely to have a cover featuring an embossed gold stiletto heel. The most Damian can hope for is that people will think it is autobiographical, and thus make him interesting. To avoid his 'I'm writing a novel' conversation, even his fellow Procrastinators congregate at the other end of the bar. Too many of them could reply, pace Peter Cook, 'Neither am I'.

Damian thinks he's the only one who's ever suffered from literary angst: 'I can feel the dormant story gnawing in my guts like a tapeworm, coiling and multiplying. My ideas burst around in my head – hey, another claret, Isidore – I'm talking *Brideshead* meets *Ulysses* meets *The Beach*.' This is stirring stuff for someone who hasn't yet written a word beyond 'The' and spent the morning agonising whether it should be 'A'. Nor has Damian a title – he's toying with *The Recondite Serpent* - agent or publisher. His short story was even rejected by a website. Damian's tiny private income is barely enough to sustain him in claret and takeaways; he wants to be lunched at The Garrick, lionised at Frankfurt. Meanwhile, there's that tricky first sentence...

The Colonial Couple

Sir edward mainwaring was rather a success in Malaysia. His father survived the Burma Road, so he felt a kinship with the Far East, dontchaknow? Marvellous people. 'Elizabeth's mother was in a Japanese camp after the fall of Singapore. Not quite Tenko, I'm glad to say, but we both had a connection. The British High Commission's in Kuala Lumpur – jolly old KL – but the seat of the federal government is in Putrajaya. I say, the sun's over the yardarm, what about a gin? No? Perhaps a vodkatonk?'

Elizabeth rootles in the herbaceous border while Edward discourses on the privilege of being in KL when Malaysia was the largest producer of tin, rubber and palm oil in the world.

'We were in India before, fascinating, but our Labs always wanted to play with the cobras in the garden. We lost Jorrocks in the first week. Then there were the gap-year idiots always having their passports stolen, and the mothers claiming they'd been at school with Elizabeth and asking us to have their spawn to stay. Do their laundry, more like. Nice to deal with a bit of manufacturing; KL was buzzing when we left.'

Edward and Elizabeth have retired to a farmhouse in Devon on the family estate. The big house is now a prep school but they're delighted not to be dealing with icy draughts and an insatiable oil bill. The garden's cobra-free and their books are delivered in brown paper parcels from Heywood Hill. Jacqui from the village is not exactly the equivalent of the dear Malay staff at the High Com, and she drives a smarter car than the Mainwarings, but Elizabeth doesn't believe in pointless luxury. They only stay with friends, never in hotels. One's been to the Oriental in Bangkok and it was so frightfully good, why bother with another?

Sir Edward gives spirited talks on headhunters in Borneo in aid of St Mary's Church; Lady Mainwaring is the soul of grace at the fête, waving a sun-spotted arm in admiration of the local publican's marrow. This is their England of sweet peas and minty Pimm's, perfect in August; in February they yearn for the South China Sea.

The Cold House

CASPER AND JEMIMA feared the worst when Mimi opened the door of Rose Cottage wearing a Puffa jacket. Never trust a hostess who is sporting outdoor clothing inside. 'Darlings! How absolutely wonderful to see you. Were my directions all right? You really can't miss us if you turn left by the yew tree after the Blind Beggar.' The yew tree was impossible to identify in the dark and the natives in the Blind Beggar had said, 'Would that be the townie couple who've rented? Hope you've got your wellies – no damp course in Rose Cottage.' A mile up a cart track they came on the idyll. The frosted condensation on the windows was a giveaway.

Mimi shepherds them into the drawing room, where they can't sit on the sofa because the dogs have first pick. Casper and Jemima perch in the fireplace, the sort of fire that draws all the heat up the chimney, having seared the bottom but left the embonpoint in a polar zone. 'You are gorgeous to come,' Mimi chirrups. 'Hugo is longing for help with the garden tomorrow.' This was not Casper's idea of a bucolic weekend reading Nicky Haslam's memoir. Jemima says gamely, 'Is there a local farm shop? I'd love to get lunch.' Mimi is adamant. 'Hugo won't go to the farm shop; so expensive. He shot the muntjac for our shepherd's pie tonight in the garden. It was eating the hebes. Hunter-gatherers, that's us! Now, darling Jem, I do advise putting these hotties in your bed so it's all toasty when you fall in after several large glasses of Hugo's best screwtop.' Jemima's heart sinks: no electric blanket. The bathroom is the contradiction of global warming. The boiler's dodgy, so tepid brown liquid hiccups sporadically from the tap. 'Lucky us, we got some oil yesterday; the Aga gulps it!' Casper and Jemima cling to the Aga as no wreckage has been clung to since the *Titanic*. Hugo is gung-ho: 'Central heating's frightfully bad for one. Why are you wearing that pashionatta thing, Jem? Are you cold?' In the bedroom, Jem bungs her hairdryer down the bed to expel the damp. Then she and Casper fluff up the rug and put it over the duvet.

The Indomitable Cyclist

Miss plummer is the stalwart of Stoke Lovage. As long as she can be seen on her sturdy bicycle, wending her way to the parochial council meeting, there'll always be an England. The bicycle is called Gertrude. Same one, sit-up-and-beg, that Miss Plummer had when she was at Girton reading English. Jolly good old friend, as is Bertie, the furry presence in the basket up front. 'As long as I've got Bertie and Gertie I'm right as a Ribston Pippin,' Miss Plummer says.

A wire basket welded to Gertrude's rear by the blacksmith contains Miss P's handbag and choice purchases from the farmers' market. There's nothing Miss Plummer cannot do with root vegetables: her parsnip chutney is a highlight of the church fête, her onion relish prized with a Christmas ham. 'Good morning, Fred, and what have we got from Home Farm today? I made an excellent jelly from your windfall apples, so here's a pot for Mrs Fred.' Then she cycles home to Honeysuckle Cottage, rejoicing in the crisp autumn morning. It's a lengthy journey as so many people stop her saying, 'Hello Miss Plummer, hello Bertie – now, I was wondering if ...' Miss Plummer (never Joyce) is importuned for everything from asking the vicar not to give such a long sermon during the family service to how to make Seville orange marmalade. 'Delia!' she booms. 'The sainted Delia. You can goggle the receipt.' Miss Plummer comes from the age of the receipt, not the recipe, and goggles not Googles. She is a demon goggler, in fact rather a whizz on the internet – Amazon's such a marvel for books – plus regular email correspondence with her niece in Tasmania. 'Sounds a spiffing place, no cars on the road, splendid food and wine, rainy mountains, like an antipodean Wales.' She intends to visit – 'One cannot spend all of one's life in this other Eden, this Cranford of Stoke Lovage' – but the vicar might get totally out of control. Salisbury is as far as Miss Plummer feels safe in venturing without his abandoning the Book of Common Prayer behind her back. At which point Bertie would bite his ankles and Miss Plummer whack him with her bicycle pump.

The Lenten Sacrifice

RODDY HAS JUST sunk into a chair and now his host is waving Château Palmer in front of him.

Well, I say! Not every day one is offering such a tiptop treat; I mean, surely a chap can make an exception? But Avril is hissing over his shoulder that Lent means Lent, and there's only a week to go and he's been a jolly good boy, so no falling at the final fence.

Roddy has bitterly regretted giving up the booze ever since noon on Ash Wednesday, normally the time for a cracking sherry and a session with the *Racing Post*. He said to Avril, who's also forsworn naughty beverages in solidarity, that surely it would be all right just to give up wine? That would be just the one nourishing Amontillado and a little whisky in the evening?

Avril was adamant: all or nothing – 'And sherry is a wine, dear.' She has hidden the bottles Away from Temptation. Roddy said that he distinctly remembered from school that one got a bit of a breather on Sundays, that Sundays were neutral territory, and one couldn't be expected to have the roast beef of old England without dignifying it with a claret. Avril opined that she doubted Stonyhurst, a byword for Catholic brutalism, was so morally lax as to allow the boys to sin by default on Sundays.

Then there was the matter of Biffy Plumptre's seventieth birthday party. 'Avril, surely we have to be a bit celebratory? Oldest friend, our best man, not going to be seventy again, always has damn good wine – it's our duty to imbibe his hospitality.' Avril was thinlipped on this one. 'Well,' she said with a disapproving sniff, 'it'll be the slippery slope. Next you'll be gulping Bordeaux on Wednesdays because you've got halfway through the week, and savaging the Sancerre on Fridays because it's the weekend. Where will it all end?'

Roddy is hopeful Lent will end very soon; he's sick of ginger beer, waving the Château Palmer away in favour of Château Tap is going to break his heart, and other people's winey breath smells ghastly when one's not drinking. 'Avril, why don't you go and police your mother for a few days?'

The Early/Late Couple

OLIVIA HAS BEEN standing in the hall for twenty minutes. She has issued the usual diktats to William about 'We cannot be late' and 'You've no idea the trouble Celia Montmorency has been to arranging Bertie's surprise sixtieth. We have to be there before he arrives.' Olivia had her hair blow-dried and sculpted at 8.30 in the morning; her matching dress and shoes were respectively pressed and polished and laid out on her bed by lunch; at teatime she had a cup of Lapsang Souchong, a bath, and made her face up with Crème de la Mer Teinte Fluide.

She wrapped Bertie's present last week and ordered the cab for 6.30 p.m. to factor in William's congenital unpunctuality and combat any problems bloody Boris might have conjured up with the traffic. Man's a useless mayor.

She has read two chapters of Nancy Mitford, so calming that she always keeps a volume on the table to while away the hours of her marriage William has spent falling about in his dressing room in wonder that time's winged chariot has brought him to a pass where he cannot find his silk evening socks. She has replied with equanimity to his howls from upstairs about also having lost his bow-tie – 'Third drawer down, left-hand side, dear' – and made sure her nails (now tensely clutching the house keys poised for departure) are quite dry. Any further imprecations beseeching 'Darling, are you ready?', 'We must go' or 'William?' yelled up the stairs fall on his selectively deaf ears. Now William Oddsocks is patting himself, desperately seeking his wallet and his mobile. 'William, I have the money for the taxi home. We are going to the Ritz, not Outer Mongolia. You don't need money since Ceci is highly unlikely to have a tombola and you are not, I trust, going to spend the evening on your mobile.' Then the eyeroll and the dangerous quiet small voice – 'If we do not get into the taxi now We Shall Be Late.' They are the first to arrive.

The Lady Taxi Driver

JANICE STANDS NO nonsense. No drunken yobs and no fornication in the back of her cab. And only foreigners up to a point. The Russians, now they're a one and no mistake. No tips and not so much as a thank you.

The Americans, now they were lovely. Don't come any more 'cos of the wobbly dollar, but they didn't know how lucky they were with Janice. She never took them on the long route, and frequently told them they'd tipped too much and handed back the excess. The poor things never seemed to get a hang of the currency.

Janice is used to pathetic gratitude. The girls, a bit tiddly outside a nightclub, who need to get home and feel safe with a woman driver: 'I'll take you, love, but don't be sick in my cab as that'll be £50 extra for the cleaning.' The old ladies tottering out of Peter Jones who need to get back to chill mansion flats: 'Don't you worry, dearie, I'll help you with those bags.'

Janice, decked in junk jewellery (one must keep up appearances), may look like a stern version of Bet Lynch, but she has her values. Do as you would be done by. She's in this job to help people; it's her independence, see? She's got a nice house in Spain from the earnings; it used to be the Costa Nothing but what with inflation it's a bit spenny, though the grandchildren love it.

Janice was a mum at nineteen in the East End, divorced the brickie husband (but they're still friendly) and the kids are in top jobs: daughter a solicitor, son a hedge funder. A bit of the old sangria and tapas is just the family ticket. Janice will move permanently when the Queen – God Bless Her – croaks and that David Cameron has made us all one big society.

Discipline, that's what this country needs. Her parents' house wasn't bombed for layabouts to drink themselves senseless and sit on their obese bottoms watching daytime telly, taking handouts from the state. 'That's you and me, love, our money. Now, shall we just call it a tenner? And don't worry, I'll stay here until you're safely through the door.'

The Antique Dealers

EILEEN AND DERMOT are united in gloom. Things are not as they were in the gentle environs of Chipping Arden, where relieving grateful Americans of their dollars for brown furniture with quite the wrong handles was the village pastime. The countess used to bring her house party to Wrootle and Rummidge for a divertissement on a Saturday morning, but now they'd all rather go to Daylesford Organic. A pot of rhubarb chutney handwoven by Lady Bamford is worth more than a stuffed Pomeranian under a glass dome.

Dermot was inspired to become an antiques dealer by John Tregorran in *The Archers*; so soothing to buy a Queen Anne bureau for £28 at the local country house sale, change the bun feet for claw feet and pop it on for £40. Now there are no country house sales and the Youth of Today, perfectly nice young marrieds, abhor brown furniture in favour of Ikea. No Queen Anne bureau ever came in a flatpack.

Eileen has thus taken to decorative. She has a contact at Colefax & Fowler with an inexhaustible demand for broken-nosed Roman emperors, putti and garden statuary of Eros. Hopefully darling John Carter will take the ornamental pillar for a creative flower arrangement at a popstar party.

'Dermot, stop mourning the eclipse of the Chippendale chair and think urns.' She's just done a very nice deal on a matching lead pair for Mrs Aspirant's patio.

Not the same sort of customer now; once Mrs Buntrock, the buyer from Bloomingdale's, used to come. That golden eagle would have been heading to a Fifth Avenue apartment, together with the finest tallboys, four chandeliers and a Georgian sideboard. Now she and Dermot drive a van to France and return with the distressed look applying to both their faces and the flaky grey-white furniture, plus four restorative cases of Château Calapso.

Dermot rubs the furniture down with wire wool, and a nice set painter from the RSC comes and makes it look vintage. It goes brilliantly with the Youth of Today's Cath Kidston binge. 'Dermot, let's sell the church font as a retro basin.'

The Non-Smoker

ALICE FEELS JUST like the goodygoody schoolgirl. 'Alice, darling, be a love and watch our bags while we nip out for a ciggie, will you?' Suddenly the table is deserted, the cool gang are screeching with laughter outside and Alice feels exactly as she did in the fifth form when she told the fun girls not to sneak down the fire escape to meet the village boys. Now, trying not to look abandoned, she is texting her mother: 'Having a super evening with Jinx, Annabel and Charlie in Peccadillos.' Her mother worries about her when she's not worrying about her Pekingese's slipped disc. 'Alice, you are so serious – could you just pick up Lotus, dear, and put her on the sofa? – your father and I are most concerned about your decision to teach in a comprehensive. You might be knifed in geography by feral youth.' Alice explains that someone has to commit to the state system. 'But it doesn't have to be you, dear. Lotus wants to get downies now, don't you Lotus?' When Annabel leads the team back in they're all giggly and faux-contrite.

'You're not going to give us a schoolteacher lecture are you? Did you order more wine?' Alice says with rare asperity that she was so busy keeping her eyes on the bags and coats that she failed to catch the eye of the waiter. Everyone says it was really nice of her, which makes Alice feel more furious about being left out.

She never was any good at smoking, although she did try at loathsome teenage parties. But her hair smelled and it was such a palaver getting rid of the butts in friends' mothers' herbaceous borders. Yet now she's being made to feel guilty at not inviting death by cancer, or pneumonia caught on a chilly pavement. Also grumpy, as the others try frightfully hard. 'Is school really scary, Alice? We think you're so brave. Awesome, here's Charlie with the wine' – visible relief all round – 'and he's got this hilarious joke about Simon Cowell. Charlie, you tell ...' Alice isn't quite up to Simon Cowell after her lonely vigil. She blames the anti-smoking police for making her feel a dead bore.

The News Junkie

Ben cannot resist a good snippet of gloom. Declining fish stocks, dirty bombs, immigration amounting to three new Birminghams (that was a very bad morning): all contribute to his belief that we're all going to hell in a handbasket. Ben is Richard Littlejohn's soulmate in the shires. Politicians? Don't make him laugh. Head Boy Cameron and his fag Clegg – does Lord Snooty Osborne add up? Global warming? The polar bears would have welcome to have a freezing holiday in his garden during June. Sometimes Ben feels he and Jeremy Paxman are the only sane men left in the world. The *Today* programme kickstarts his day with enough indignation to get him out of bed and united with the cafetiere. That's after much of the night spent with the BBC World Service; Ben was with hostage Alan Johnson in spirit every one of his 114 days in captivity. Johnson's release kept Ben gripped to *BBC News 24*. He loves a rolling news story: 9/11, 7/7, the tsunami – he was straight on to Sky. Failing a horrible train crash or natural disaster he can reliably find a depressing article about the extinction of tigers (*Daily Telegraph*) or the painful extraction of bears' bile by the Chinese (*Daily Mail*) to make his day. Ben's wife Rosie, a merry soul, says why doesn't he listen to classical music and take up reading? So much more soothing. Unfortunately Ben hit on Wagner, which was too much *Sturm und Drang* even for him, and Simon Sebag Montefiore's *Young Stalin* has just convinced him there's a rotter screaming to get out of anyone given half a chance. The only light on the horizon of a morning spent with newspaper columnists dissecting the lumpen gravitas of Mr Brown's government is Martha Kearney. Her silken authority on *The World at One* is balm to a troubled soul.

Unlike Huw Edwards at ten o'clock, who Ben wants to slap. To think this lightweight is apparently going to commentate at the Queen's funeral! Not that Ben has anything against Welshmen. Only by signing off with Rottweiler Paxman can Ben sleep easy in his bed.

The Social Asset

VIOLET MET GNASHER in the park. Violet's mama was a bit worried about Gnasher – he seemed so big and Violet is such a delicate blossom – but Tony, Gnasher's dad, said 'Don't you worry, missus. Gnasher wouldn't hurt a fly and he's a real gentleman with the ladies.' Indeed Gnasher is, and very protective of Violet should any of the council estate pitbull-alikes menace her. 'They all look horridly fierce to me,' says Violet's mama. But Tony says, 'Look here, Winifred,' – they're on Winifred and Tony terms after several companionable walkies – 'you've gotta understand there are no bad dogs, only bad owners. The yoof of today is what you wanna avoid. I never come into the park after m'dinner' – Winifred does a quick translation into lunch – 'The yoof is out with its pitbulls after a nice lie-in, having spent all night burgling yer house, like.' They both laugh, and Tony gives Violet and Gnasher a Happy Walkie treat. Winifred says it must be rather dreadful living in a tower block, particularly for the dogs. Tony agrees. 'Shouldn't be allowed, I say.' Gnasher and Violet, Winifred and Tony continue in happy accord past the statue of a hero of Waterloo. 'Lost his leg, y'know, blown off while he was on that horse,' says Tony, 'but he just said to the Duke of Wellington, "Don't worry, sir, I've got another one." He meant his leg, not the horse, although I expect he had a few more of those, poor sod.' Violet and Winifred are most impressed by Tony's knowledge of Lord Uxbridge's travails.

Violet, whose eyes are a bit sharper than Winifred's, looks out for Gnasher and Tony every morning. They feel safe together and Winifred confides that her father had an awful war – 'Jap concentration camp. Burma Road. Bit frail after that' – and, patting Violet, realizes she's never talked about it before. 'I say, Winifred, I've got a little council flat – thank you, Mrs Thatcher – with a garden for Violet and Gnasher. Would you like to come and have a nice cup of tea, love?' Gnasher wags, Violet bounces, Winifred says how very kind. They're not lonely anymore.

The Conceptual Artist

FREDERICK LOOKS LIKE a banker. But if you understood post-image you'd realize his suit and his handmade suede shoes were ironic. Frederick believes in his own self-contained universe of myth, autobiography, metamorphosis and iconoclasm. Frederick conceives the mystical association of disparate objects. Frederick, or rather Frederick's business-like factory of installation engineers, floated a packet of Marlboro, a photostat of Michelangelo's David, three cheese straws and a Penguin classic of *Lady Chatterley's Lover* in a Perspex frame and called it 'Go Figure?'. It's now in a museum in Philadelphia, where the good citizens are too frightened to admit they don't understand it. Frederick's Tate Liverpool triumph has been a wall of opaque glass etched with the words Obsessive, Air-Kiss, Temporality, War-Torn, Vitreous and Apocalyptic. It is colour-washed with revolving lime-green and violet light, with an hourly display of fractured black dots representing bullet holes flowering into plants to signify the renewable power of nature. Frederick designed it on his laptop.

Frederick has been begged by the *Guardian* for his views on this year's Turner Prize. He's raised a plucked eyebrow of dismissal in the Gore Vidal manner of 'It is not enough to succeed, others must fail', yet been exquisitely pungent within hearing of diary columnists. 'Goshka Macuga might worship at the shrine of Paul Nash but cut-out images of luminously plumed turkeys do not work for me with wrecked airplane fusilage. You know she shamelessly raided the Tate archive? Hardly original work.'

At lunch at Quo Vadis, over the native oysters, Frederick wonders to his agent whether he should design Christmas wrapping paper. 'Mark Wallinger did marvellously writing Jesus Christ on paper; it was a vibrant statement against the consumerist Santa thing.' His agent is only grateful Frederick hasn't opted for Vaseline and the Matthew Barney video-performance concept of putting ice screws up his bottom. It would ruin the suit.

The Old Flirts

VIVIEN AND MAURICE met over the dahlias at the Dower House garden open day. Maurice gave Vivien a terrific twinkle and ventured that he could never make his mind up whether dahlias were marvellous or frightfully non-U, and Vivien had replied, 'Frightfully non-U, which is why they're so marvellous.' Twin souls, they repaired to the tea tent. Vivien said how jolly it was to see a chap in a proper panama, and Maurice gallantly popped the ball back over the net with, 'Your hat's quite a stunner. Last saw hats like that worn by coolies when I was in China. Looks much better on you, my dear.' Maurice and Vivien have since met at the Woolpit for lunch. Vivien ordered the grilled plaice – 'No wonder you've got such a fine figure, if I may say so, ma'am' – and Maurice the fish pie and a bottle of Sancerre; both approve of the advent of gastropubs. 'Great improvement on the Chateau Gutrot and chips of yore. Now, Vivien, do you like musical theatre?' Vivien does.

They discover a mutual love of the classics: *Top Hat, My Fair Lady, South Pacific, Anything Goes*: 'There was a splendid production at Grange Park, Maurice. I can't think why they've given up musicals in favour of charmless obscure operas.' Would it be too risqué to venture to London for a matinee of *Oliver!*? Vivien thinks they might have to take a grandchild as cover.

'Surely you're far too young to be a grandmother!' says Maurice gallantly, but Vivien confesses to five grandchildren, which he can match with 'six of the little blighters. Love teaching them to play chess. Young Freddie can beat me now.' He is a widower, she a divorcée (Maurice wonders what chump would let this fascinator go); both have impractical cottages with too many stairs, according to their children who've confined them to senility. If they saw Maurice tempting Vivien with the gooseberry fool – 'Or shall we share the platter of local artisan cheeses?' – they'd be rather shocked by the sprightliness of it all, with Vivien's magnifying glass in full flirt mode, reading glasses being far too old lady. Who knows where it will all go?

The British Holiday

DAD GRASPED THE nettle in the Easter hols. 'Well, Jamie, Rose, Emily, the thing is, er, that we won't be going to Corfu in the summer. Credit crunch, strength of the euro, things a bit dicey for me at work I'm afraid.' His little Emily had hugged him and said she didn't mind a bit. Jamie had pulled a face; he'd really, really been looking forward to hanging out in Kassiopi with the rest of Radley, Stowe and Eton. Rose, the family swot, said she'd read a newspaper article about staycations and home being the new away. Then Mummy said brightly that it was really brilliant: 'Uncle Edwin's going to lend us his house on the west coast of Scotland – picnics, boats, that lovely beach with the white sand.' Rose thought Famous Five with midges; Jamie thought 'No PlayStation'; Emily thought car sick on the eight-hour drive. Dim memories of Uncle Edwin's house included it being so damp that Jamie had had to sleep in his wetsuit.

Yet here they all are having rather a good time. Mummy is thrilled that she's been able to bring the dogs and can listen to *The Archers*; Dad can get the *Daily Telegraph* on the right day; Jamie has been allowed to bring a friend; Rose is reading *Gone With the Wind*. No child is bollocked for staying in bed until lunch time with Dad roaring, 'I'm paying for this holiday so you'll bloody well get up and enjoy it.' Emily, bless her little heart, makes friends with the curmudgeonly Rayburn and coaxes shepherd's pie out of it. She and her dad are whiz at playing Vingt-et-un. Jamie and his mate, having survived the shock of no Sky TV or mobile reception, disappear to play boats and achieve outstanding mackerel fishing. The first results were grilled on an instant tinfoil barbecue acquired from Mrs McTavish in the village shop. Now Jamie and Dad have dug a barbecue pit and are immolating legs of lamb and baked potatoes. Mum hisses, 'Don't mention Boy Scout!'; Rose walks the dogs – moony rambles in which she daydreams of Rhett Butler. All have been spared airport chaos due to strike action.

The Milkman

JOSH CAN REMEMBER a time when being a milkman was about real milk, not semi-skimmed or organic or skinny. Orange juice was the beginning of the slippery slide towards butter, cheese and yogurt. His little white van is now groaning with pomegranate, blueberry and acai smoothies, bread (white, wholewheat and seeded batch loaves), tea bags, even water (fizzy and still). Josh's dad would have died laughing – if he wasn't already on the milk round in the sky – at the idea of a milkman delivering water.

But Josh's bosses at Dairy Fresh say diversification is the only way to keep business going.

So Josh now delivers Go-Kat to Mrs Pettifer and grow-bags to the gent at Polecat Cottage, who loves his tomatoes. It's a good excuse to check up on the old dears; Josh has had his moments finding customers prone on the kitchen floor and done his bit with 999.

Mrs Pettifer leaves her key under the flowerpot and asks Josh to check the fridge and see what she needs. The professional couples in the louvre-shuttered second homes communicate with Josh online the night before, requesting sugarless muesli, fat-free yogurt and the *Guardian*.

Josh delivers all the newspapers – nice little earner.

He's currently got an enterprising offer on bedding plants: £2 for six begonias, busy lizzies or virulent orange marigolds. And he'll do you compost and fertilizer; just send him a text on the mobile.

Josh is a mini-Ocado in his patch of Suffolk. Sitting down with Lady Posset for a rare cuppa – 'I don't have the time any more, having to deliver all the vegetables' – he confides that he once wanted to be East Anglia's answer to Dean Martin. Which, as Lady Posset tells Sir Peregrine Posset, explains the Ted hair.

As the van trundles off down the gravel, she admires the Darwinian adaptation of this pillar of the community to modern times. 'The diversification lark's got Bonios and budgie food next to my double cream, Lady P. It'll be yer Bolly next.' Sir Peregrine wonders if Josh could deliver sherry.

Decorating the Church

Eileen batterham has been doing hideous things to the font with berries and chrysanths for twenty Christmases. She is certainly not going to be told by Rowena, a mere newcomer to the Manor Farmhouse, not to smoke in the vaulting, chill vastness of St Mary's. Rowena, so eager to help, has entirely failed to grasp the rigid order of precedence re windowledge and pew.

She offered to hold a ladder for Mrs Cripswell, who does things with poinsettias to the ledge behind the altar, in front of the stained-glass nativity scene, but was firmly told, 'I may have had two hip operations, dear, but I am perfectly capable.'

Rowena humbly held greenery for Mrs Sherrin, who has the arrangement by the lectern. Fortified by blood-red dahlias, it is rigid, like sticky-out arms and legs. Mrs Sherrin was inducted into the triangular method of flower design at Winkfield in the 1960s and she's not going to change now.

Nice Susie who, after ten years in the Chantry House, has been allowed to do the back windowsill, is dithering between her holly and her ivy. Rowena says there's a socket 'just there' and wouldn't it be lovely to have fairy lights woven in with Susie's greenery? As her still small suggestion of festivity rings up the aisle, the collective breath of the flower ladies exhales in little clouds. Fairy lights?

This is St Mary's, not Santa's Grotto at Harrods. It is quite enough that Violet Mayfield, whose parents-in-law have only lived here since the last war, has given 200 night lights, which are so tiresome for the church wardens to light. Last year there was the tricky business of the new Polish family donating a battery-operated fibre-optic wreath for the church door.

Susie (who thinks fairy lights would be a heavenly lift to her sad little effort) gives Rowena a hug – as much as is possible through their layers of polar clothing – and says, 'Don't worry about old Eileen Battering-Ram; she's really a duck. And in the end it all looks marvellous.'

The Professional Mourners

MADGE WAS EAGLE-EYED. From the time Sir Cedric Thespian's death was announced on Radio 4 she scanned the *Court & Social* for the memorial service. Hurrah! The Actors' Church at noon on a Thursday. Being a pro, Madge instantly wrote with a stamped addressed envelope (much more likely to secure tickets, in her long mourning experience, for people she doesn't know) requesting a pair for herself and Hilda. It'll be such a nice day out, travelling up from Bletchworth on their senior citizen rail passes.

They'll have a racy cup of coffee in Covent Garden (the prices!) and then a free performance from Dame Judi Dench reading a Shakespeare sonnet, perhaps Sir Donald Sinden rumbling a poem, a eulogy from Alan Bennett, a reading by Penelope Keith and a song by Elaine Paige. Oooh, 'Memories'!

Madge and Hilda always arrive early for a good memorial so that they can catch the stars on the way in. Madge is fearless about thrusting her autograph book forward. 'Lovely to see you, Miss Paige. You wouldn't mind, would you?' Hilda is just so happy to star-spot. 'Isn't that Prunella Scales or maybe June Whitfield?' Madge says, 'No dear, it's the Queen – that's what Prunella Scales played at the National when we went to a matinee.'

Madge and Hilda attended Lord Olivier's memorial at Westminster Abbey and that of Dame Peggy Ashcroft. 'We like to see the stars in their natural state,' they say, as if the dames were in grassy enclosures at Whipsnade. Madge thinks she once saw Prince Charles embracing Dame Judi.

Fellow anoraks in standing-room-only whinge. 'Well, I don't know why they didn't have it in a bigger church. Cedders was a beloved figure, an icon – did you hear him on *Subterfuge*? I never missed it in twenty years – and I saw every one of his shows, including the one about the drunk played by Lawrence of Arabia. Honestly, I don't know why they didn't have this in a theatre.'

As the congregation rises for 'Guide Me, O Thou Great Redeemer', Madge is devoting rodent cunning to crashing the wake at The Garrick.

The Gap Year 2010

Isabella is on Facebook to her besties from Downe House and Eton, recording her status: 'Just got to Koh Samui with Lulu, Roo and Harry. Cool! Who's up for the Full Moon Party on Koh Phangan?' Lulu is texting, Harry is downloading his photos, Roo – who has grown a parent-defying topknot while gapping – is having a few beers. They're travelling in a pod (honestly, duh, Apple should invent iGap) and whenever they've landed in Australia/Vietnam/Cambodia/Hong Kong the first thing they do after dumping rucksacks of unironed clothes in the Three Cockroach Youth Hostel is hit the internet cafe. They may not be sure whether they are in Vietnam, Cambodia, Hong Kong or Australia (clue here is that the natives speak a version of English) but they are ostensibly travelling to different places while meeting exactly the same people. 'Sophie! Yay! You're at the Yum Yum Snake Sinbin? With Poppy and Lucas!? Awesome. C u 2nite at Soi Green Mango, babe.' Their parents do not know whether to be grateful that their children are electronically tagged or desperate that the round the world ticket blagged from godparents as an eighteenth birthday present is being abused by drinking Cosmos made with – well, who the hell knows what they're made with? Then there was the terrible story of Charlie Edge who was zapped by a black mamba in South Africa. The *Daily Mail* likes nothing better than the exotic gappy death. All gap mothers are in meltdown every time the telephone rings. 'Hi, Mum! I'm fine. Lucy, Tinky, Squeezy and Milly are here in Hanoi; it's so great. Love you.' At the internet cafe they are shamelessly confident. 'Come on, Izzy. Your dad knows the Brit Con. We'll put on our Docksiders and Mr Pink shirts and surely they'll give us the full decent meal.' Izzy facebooks everyone saying, 'See you, darlings, at Haad Rin Nok – it's the party beach! Love you! Then we can all dive with whale sharks.'

Back home the parents say, 'Of course Isabella is going to teach English to sweet little Nepalese people – her gap isn't all fun, you know,' and, 'Roo is giving his time to rehabilitate giant catfish in the Mekong.'

The Ancient Volunteer

Moira is delighted that Christmas is over and she can get back to the Emily Austen House. At home the dog has savaged the tinsel and the larder is a chamber of horrors: the drying turkey carcase, a suppurating ham, very dead mince pies made by Aunt Heather. The dishwasher has gone on the blink. Here, with Emily, Moira feels truly at home.

There is order, there are her flowers which she did herself, tastefully in green and snowberries. The poinsettia has not darkened the door of the Emily Austen House under Moira's watch. Her make-up, her hat and her wig (post-chemo) are all in their place and, despite her having been ill, nothing cheers her more than these days in the peace of literature.

She is a benefactor of the Emily Austen Foundation, which has a splendid transatlantic relationship with the College of William and Mary in Williamsburg, Virginia, established 1693. 'A year before the Bank of England but by the same people,' as Moira tells the cognoscenti. She does few conducted tours these days – a bit tiring – but her Elizabeth Arden smile and her immaculate manicure handing over the leaflets ('Now, I do think it would be fun for you to have a little guide') impress the aspirant literary visitor with the promise of style.

'I saw the adaptation of *Single and Singularity* on the BBC, or was it *Bridget Jones*? Y'know the one about the girl who seeks love?' And Moira says drily, 'That is what we are all seeking, madam, do enjoy your tour.' There is a surge every time an Emily Austen film comes out. 'Did Keira really come here?' 'No, madam, it was made on the Yorkshire moors; that is where the novel is set.' 'So no Keira, then? Right, Tracy, we're going home now.' Sometimes Moira wonders why she bothers.

But there are so many who follow the brown sign to the Emily Austen House and are thrilled by the garden and the library's first editions, and don't expect Mrs Benedict to come bursting into the panelled drawing room demanding husbands for her daughters.

At the end of the day Moira snaps her crocodile handbag shut and, as a widow, returns to the ham that no husband will carve.

The Opera Hater

PUFFER IS IN torment. Had the Gestapo got their mitts on him during the war, one blast of Wagner and he'd have told them everything. Opera is torture. Dear Patricia loves it, so his married life, otherwise so sanguine, has been blighted by trips to Glyndebourne and Garsington (with the added threat in recent years of The Grange) during which he has counted down the minutes until the picnic.

Puffer's pretty much got the old girl trained to go to the Royal Opera House with a chum, although he was dragged to *Rigoletto* by the Montmorencys. Pretty startling stuff, that duke was a shocker, what with topless hussies, and Puffer doesn't even want to think about the chaps' extraordinary goings on with other chaps. Only time he hasn't fallen asleep in the first act. He thought he cracked rather a good joke about 'La Donna e Mobile' being an aria for a lost phone, but Patricia looked thunderous.

Now they're at Charlie Plunkett's seventieth birthday. Charlie and Amelia are mightily pleased with themselves for getting Trinket Opera to perform *La Traviata* in their drawing room. Puffer knows *La Traviata* – it's the one where that bloody woman takes hours to die. He has moved his little gilt chair to a far, solitary corner. Before proceedings commenced, he took the precaution of downing a large amount of Charlie's champagne, and sandwiching multiple coy bits of smoked salmon together in the hope that food coma will summon Nepenthe to soothe the fevered brow. He is now coiled in a Gordian knot of frustration, longing to tell Violetta that if she's got such a damned cough she should take a Strepsil and brace up. Time has slowed to a standstill. Will anyone notice if he slinks out for a cigarette (hence Puffer)? Oh for the days when entertainment meant going to a John Wayne film at the local Empire, and seeing that romantic stream of smoke rising through the projection beam. The trouble with opera is that it's just too grand.

The Frantic Retirement

PEEPS AND CHUBBY have never been so busy since they retired. Peeps is Lady Captain of the Micklethwaite Golf Club; Chubby is giving the vicar hell on the PCC. 'We'll have no happy-clappy nonsense at St Mary's and we absolutely don't do the sign of peace.' There's Peeps' book group every second Thursday of the month, bridge on Tuesdays, pilates in the village hall – 'Don't want to fall to bits now we've got all this lovely time' – and Chubby's project for the restoration of the village pond.

Their diaries are a nightmare. Wine and nibbles in aid of the Conservatives (Peeps contributes her famous cheese puffs); the Bach recital at the cathedral; a private visit to see the rhododendrons at Exbury with the Horticultural Circle. Chubby is doing a computer course, although he says his grandson is a better teacher than the spotty chap at the sixth form college. The joys of Amazon are now his, and he's got the hang of Google. 'Chubby's quite the techno-whizz,' Peeps tells her church flower rota. 'He's researching classical Turkey and wants us to go on a cruise.'

The windows of opportunity are limited between Peeps' attendance at the Anthony Trollope Writing Conference and Chubby's monthly luncheon at the Scalded Cat with Godfrey, Jasper and Hamish. 'Can't miss that, old girl – got to keep on top of the gossip and Godders is bringing his laptop with pictures of Leptis Magna. Downloaded them from his digital thingy; gone to a lot of trouble.' Then there's the Van Gogh exhibition, which they're combining with a visit to the theatre. 'Marvellous things, these old people's rail passes. We just pop up to London, we've got Freedom passes too for the Undie, and whizz about catching up on a bit of culture. I can pop into the Sloane Club for a bevvy while Peeps hits Peter Jones.' Saturday nights are always dinner parties: 'We'll be frightfully informal' means smoking jackets and four courses. Peeps is a demon for Jamie Oliver; all vegetables come from the garden and eggs from Peeps' hens. With all this frenetic activity it's surprising the dogs ever get walked at all.

The Nervous Flyer

NANCY IS CLENCHING her buttocks in the manner approved by the self-help manual on fear of flying. Clench, release. Breathe in, squeeze. Clench, release. Unwittingly she's also clutching the arm of the nice young man in the next-door seat – possibly to the extent that her manicured-for-holiday nails draw blood. There were many dangerous situations that Tom's father warned him about on his gap year, but being physically assaulted by a middle-aged woman on the outgoing flight wasn't one of them. She also keeps levitating, mysterious to one not privy to the buttock-clenching technique. The engine roar on take-off induces white knuckles. As for the safety demonstration, with the pointless advice about taking off high heels before proceeding down the exit shute 'should the aeroplane land on water'; Nancy knows they will all die. Since when has a 747 been able to float? Also, as the flight to Thailand proceeds mostly overland, wouldn't a parachute be of more use than a life jacket? Nancy cannot think why she ever agreed to go and visit her sister in Koh Samui. A happy train journey to Brittany would have been so agreeable; even a drive to Scotland necessitating departure at 3.30 a.m. to avoid congestion around Birmingham. At 33,000 ft Nancy disentangles herself from Tom, with flushed apologies, in order to have a turbo-powered gin and tonic, a stun gun poured on top of the valium she took before check-in. Normally a mild-mannered florist indulging only in creative ways with chrysanthemums, Nancy's chosen medication has a reverse thrust of making her excessively chatty. Does Tom know that statistically one is in greater peril from boiling an egg than flying? Not that this helps her fear as she never boils eggs – so constipating. Does Tom know that one person in four suffers severe anxiety at the idea of boarding a plane? That it ranks alongside fear of snakes? No, Tom doesn't know, or care, but is now developing acute claustrophobia. He pointedly puts on his headphones to block Nancy out with *Pirates of the Caribbean*; over Iran she and her balloony bosoms fall asleep against his arm. Tom clenches his buttocks.

The Poppy Seller

HAROLD HAS THE patch outside Tesco Extra in Kingsbourne. Mrs Wetherspoon was fearful of a rough element (and thus opted for a genteel stint at the Organic Food Market) but Harold said if anyone questioned what our brave boys were doing in Afghanistan he could tell them a thing or two about Johnny Taliban. Harold wasn't in 2 Para for nothing. He was one of the volunteers in the Independent Para Squad that joined 22 SAS in Malaya in 1954 to fight the Commie menace. No one asked him about Post Traumatic Stress after he'd stuck eighteen inches of bayonet through the enemy and seen his best mate dying with his guts spilling out in the dust.

So no lardy thug on benefits is going to diss the British Legion to Harold. They helped his dad, also in the Paras, when he got tinnitus after taking out the monster guns behind Sword and Juno beaches. The Normandy Landings wouldn't have been possible otherwise. Gulf War-related illness, pensions – the Legion's on your side, unlike the bloody government. Mind you, this is the environs of Sainsbury Plain, and many of the young mums with screaming Tyrone in tow are NCOs' wives, with their men in Helmand. They say, 'Come on, Tyrone, put 50p in the box now.'

Harold shows Tyrone his medals. 'That one's for Singapore, sonny. Jungle warfare in 1964. We wapped fifty of them and only lost two men.' The farmers' wives, nipping in for Finish Powerballs, say, 'Hello, Harold – damn, my poppy's on the other jacket; let's have another,' and produce a pound.

On a sunny Saturday he'll do more than £300 standing ramrod-straight in the cold wind. 'Thank you, sir,' says Harold, as a gent in red corduroys stuffs in a fiver. On Remembrance Sunday there'll be fewer veterans at the parade in Kingsbourne church, where Harold bears the British Legion flag. The old boys are dying off, but Harold will remember them.

The Whispery Dining Room

LUCRETIA AND GRAHAME have perfected exactly the right attitude of sniffy disdain essential to a food temple. Never let it be said that they are not accustomed to Puligny-Montrachet or a fine Pommard. Whatever the wine waiter suggests with the duck, Grahame will chose something quite different to flex his sophistication. Usually more expensive, which immediately gives him away as a pretentious ass. Since it is not done to speak above hushed tones, nor laugh, Lucretia and Grahame have no need to communicate, a relief to them both. He is going to have the lobster with black truffles; she, peppered tuna with a shallot jus. She eats two bites and pushes the rest around her plate with the insouciance of the joylessly thin. He hisses: 'Eat up, girl; do you know what that cost?' She doesn't, having been handed the menu with no prices. Around them there is little to hear except the crackle of starched linen. Other equally mute couples – married people – are indulging in the smart silence. Not one of the women touches the bread kneaded at dawn with water imported from France. English water produces inferior aeration according to Grahame, who unfortunately knows everything. The presence of a child in Le Grand Bouffe is as if glass has been shattered. 'Can I have chips?' reverberates around the whispery dining room like an aural Bateman cartoon. Lucretia, who doesn't have children (too fattening), hisses that if the sprog is going to be taken out as a treat surely the Zoo would be more appropriate? Then there is their silver dome moment: the reverential carrying of the vast plates with tiny amounts of cured duck pot-au-feu with herb oil (Grahame) and lamb Cleopatra (Lucretia), then the synchronized dome-lifting with the chanted description of what is on their plates: 'Madame has milk-fed baby lamb with lemon, tomatoes, artichokes and olives. For Sir, the duck with a leetle twist by Chef Defarge of fresh clams.' Lucretia, mouth pursed to the smallest aperture for admitting food, wonders why anyone thinks they can't remember what they ordered. Is it because she looks old? The childish voice rings out again: 'Papa, do they have ice cream here?' All secretly wish they had the confidence to ask.

The Homesick Child

PHOEBE WANTS M-M-MUMMY.

Sob. Phoebe wants the smell of home, wood fires and Mummy's fug of scented candles; she wants her bedroom and if she could only go home her bedroom would never be untidy again. Promise. Cross her heart and hope to die. Panda, Teddy and Ellie would rather like to go home too, if only to dry out on the Aga. They've been wept into copiously. Phoebe is not allowed a mobile for the first month at St Mary's so she can't talk to M-M-Mummy and only one letter has made it through the postal strike. The news that Moonbeam is fine, on his feed and being exercised by Sally from the village is now a crumpled talisman of all that is familiar.

Mummy hopes that Phoebe is enjoying hockey (she's not) and being a good girl (she's trying) and making lovely new friends (tricky, through the veil of tears. Ruby Hicks calls her Pheeble). 'It'll be the first exeunt in no time, darling. The dogs send wags and licks, although I do wonder about Jack Russells. Lettice ate her own bodyweight in meringue at lunch on Sunday and was sick in Daddy's shoe.' Phoebe wants her D-D-Daddy. Christabel from the sixth form found her in a sodden heap in the piano practice rooms and allowed Phoebe to use her mobile; Daddy was in a meeting but a heart-wrenching message was gulped down the telephone. So Daddy rang Miss Mincham, convinced Phoebe was being beaten and starved, and Christabel got into the most awful stink. Phoebe was really, really sorry, like, she just, like, wanted to die under her Cath Kidston duvet.

That night her house mother brought the whole dorm hot chocolate and said that because of the horrid post all the New Squirts would be allowed to email home tomorrow. 'Try not to make your parents miserable; I bet they're worrying about you like mad.' So Phoebe writes that she hopes Mummy and Moonbeam aren't lonely and she's got to go to drama now. Phoebe likes drama and Ruby Hicks is really good at it. Her parents live abroad, like, so sad. 'Dear Mummy, please may I bring Ruby home at Michaelmas exeunt? She's my best friend.'

The Duke's Mother-in-Law

NANCY LOOKS EXACTLY like an English gentlewoman, circa the era of Edward Molyneux, but being American is unlike her in any respect. Nancy's nails are manicured, instead of filled with flowerbed; her diamonds are clean and she utterly fails the Hardy Amies test: that the immutable chic of an aristocrat is that she looks as if she has just come up from the country and is about to go back there.

Nancy, aka Mrs Henry Frobisher IV, has a triplex on Park Avenue and is currently waiting for her daughter, the Duchess, at the Colony Club, so they may have luncheon in the beautiful dining room eating reassuringly disgusting food. All Nancy's clubs, from Piping Rock in Locust Valley to Lyford Cay, are the last bastions of mince. They think it is shabby chic; softshelled crabs, in season, are the only intimation of luxury and taste like deep-fried Kleenex.

Nancy does not do fancy; Swifty's is as good as it gets; she will have either the twin hamburgers or the Cobb salad, and after 9/11 went there wearing a black velvet beret sporting a tiny Stars and Stripes pin – in real diamonds, rubies and sapphires. The Astors may be her second cousins, and a flightier relation married a Rockefeller, but Nancy is quietly confident that when those rather tiresome Pilgrim Fathers landed on Plymouth Rock, her family was already in the exquisite house on Fifth Avenue that is now a museum.

What attracted the Duke of Chalfont to the $50 million Frobisher heiress? Summer Frobisher is pretty well educated (Brown) and tries hard, particularly at keeping her mother away from Chalfont House.

She is constantly flying to London – 'We're staying with our son-in-law, The Dook' – for the latest theatre, to seek the Broadway transfer that might be suitable for a benefit for her educational foundation. Nancy and Henry scour the world for culture with the Metropolitan's tours, and private visits to the Hermitage and the Sistine Chapel. They've long since given up the vulgarity of Ascot, but just love dinners at Highgrove with Charles and Camilla in aid of the Prince's Trust.

The Dangerous Dad

CLIVE IS THE dad of all dads. He's raided dodgy newsagents for under-the-counter fireworks; he's ordered rockets on line; he's forbidden Angela to recycle any cardboard or newspaper for the past month to kick start a bonfire at the bottom of the garden. For purposes of this conflagration he has trawled Spar for firelighters and service stations for logs in impossible-to-open string bags. On the great night of 5 November he will be bellow for 'Scissors, Angela! Where are you, woman? Bring the matches – no, not those matches, the long matches. Use your noddle.' Angela (responsibility, hot sausages and ketchup) can foresee a night spent in A&E, but at this moment, as Clive produces his booty, his sons think he's Hero-Dad. 'Well, Bobby and Ashley, what about this, eh? Want to invite some of your mates around for the show? I've got Midnight Werewolves, that's thirty glittering red comets with reports and crackles; I've got Martian Attack – how about that? 102 shots of colour stars with bang-bang-bangs. And Pluto rockets, a candle battery and a Shot Flashing Thunder air bomb repeater!' All the time Angela thought Clive was indulging in gainful employment, he was surfing brilliantfireworks. com, ghenghisfireworks, becoming intimate with the Chinese Fireworks Co. Ltd in Sheffield ('Fireworks for Divali, funerals and divorces – You'll be Blown Away'). Now he possesses Missile Attack, 150 shots of whistling surface-to-air missiles guaranteed to infuriate the neighbours. Angela regrets the decline of Wapshott Council's public bonfire and firework display due to Health and Safety, driving big kids like Clive underground with their bazookas. Precious little safety at 28 Cherry Blossom Avenue. Last year he burnt down the garden fence by nailing Catherine Wheels to it, and he's a one for digging a pit laboriously filled with sand from B&Q – 'Come on, boys, help me here' – and propping the more venomous fireworks in it. There's then a lot of 'Stand back, everyone' while he peers over the edge just as the rockets are getting up speed. This year Clive's pride and joy is the Ultimate Fear 4 inch mine: 'Nearly twenty decibels of pure testosterone, probably the loudest firework in England.'

The Hateful Hosts

JEREMY HAS SPENT a charmless night in the Blue Room. The bed, once slept in by Harold Macmillan when he came to address the local Conservatives, has prep school sag; the mattress is made of rocks and the pillows of concrete. Injudicious movement causes the sheets to emit sparks. Meredith Scutt-Buttle is clearly the sort of hostess who lavishes 100 per cent nylon upon her guests. So at 7 a.m. Jeremy arose, abluted (bathwater cold, towels thin, mean little soap purloined from the Miramar Hotel) and crept downstairs to make a cup of coffee: instant. Exhaustive exploration of the Scutt-Buttle kitchen failed to reveal any Fairtrade Nicaraguan fresh-ground dark roast, only a catering tin of Gold Blend.

As he contemplates Hugh Scutt-Buttle's collection of Delft and the grandfather clock strikes eight – a time when the siren smell of bacon normally wafts towards a guest's room – his hosts materialize in panic mode. Please would he sit down while drinking coffee in case of spills? Mrs Scutt-Buttle pursues him to the sofa with a duster. Jeremy sits gingerly and several moths fly out of the cushions. Hugh says, tight-lipped, 'Just enjoy your coffee, old chap. We'll rustle up brekkie.' Not much rustling for white toast and Golden Shred.

Jeremy is feeling miffed. He deluged the Scutt-Buttles with grouse and ghillies when they came to fish with him on the Findhorn. Mrs S-B was shrouded in electric blankets; Hugh had a decanter of whisky on his bedside table. Where is the kindly drinks tray at Concrete Pillow Manor? The Scutt-Buttle invitation to fish on the Test, which Jeremy went to such extravagance to secure, is rapidly losing its allure.

The other four guest rooms obdurately lack guests, so no merry house party. The fishing picnic looms as a Scotch egg and a warm can of beer. The kitchen recce revealed only a meagre saddle of lamb: presumably dinner. Jeremy is warming up (after the fishing) to a family crisis. 'Mumsie not very well, ninety now, do hope you understand.' Driving away, he wonders whether anyone had slept in his bed since Harold Macmillan.

The Fashion Student

EMILY IS LATE for her work experience at *Gloss* magazine, 'cos she was, like, in Shoreditch last night at Bistrotheque eating canteen-style upstairs. It was so cool. Then she went downstairs for lip-synching trannies, which anyone who wasn't a fashion student or aspirant Britpop artist might mistake for karaoke. Emily's breakfast has thus consisted of a Coke and two Nurofen Plus.

Today she's going with the accessories editor to the press day for a new handbag line. So she's 'borrowed', aka nicked, her mum's Vuitton. Emily, like, needs the cred; Mum's only going to Waitrose. In her babydoll top, leggings and furry coat from Brick Lane market, hair a stranger to the brush and false eyelashes half falling off, like exhausted tarantulas, Emily looks as if she's been thrown together in a tumbledrier. In fact Emily devotes most of her waking hours (which are admittedly limited) to her look; no pile of smelly old clothes, otherwise known as vintage, in Portobello goes unturned on a Saturday morning before coffee at the Electric. Mum's old Ossie Clarks have long since been 'borrowed'. She haunts Alfies Antiques Market in search of originality but sweetly ends up, in her Mary Jane shoes or ballet flats, looking just as if she's come off a production line of St Martins students, which indeed she has.

Her icons are Alexander McQueen and Christopher Kane. Emily told the fashion editor that she was sooooo into textiles: 'A bit Alexander McQueen, yer know, a bit Stella; I did a project mixing tweed with chiffon.' So far Emily's interest in textiles has manifested itself most prominently in raids on the fashion cupboard.

She's just got nothing to wear to Bungalow 8, despite Mum pointing out the heaving mass of clothes on Emily's bedroom floor. 'Oh, those ...'

All the fascinatingly original purchases are dismissed with a wave of a blue Chanel nail-varnished hand. Emily's grunge look is only fit for AKA off Tottenham Court Road – why doesn't Mum get it?

The Cat Sitter

TREVOR IS ENTIRELY happy with the lonely life of cat-sitting Ozymandias. Unlike dog-sitting, it does not involve cuddles, affection or walks. Ozymandias looks furious to see Trevor, most probably because Trevor upsets his dignity by calling him Ozzy and 'There, there, Kitty'. At which Ozymandias puts up his tail, and walks tall through the cat flap.

Trevor is content in the house heavy with empty silence. He has inspected the McPhees' family photographs in the drawing room, and established from the bookshelves that his employers are Frederick Forsyth and Penny Vincenzi paperback sorts of people. They are on an autumn break playing tennis in Marbella, and Joan McPhee texts Trevor constantly with enquiries as to whether Ozymandias is eating his tinned salmon. Also handy advice such as 'O's cage in cellar if u hve 2 take him 2 vet.'

A laminated diet sheet for Ozymandias, plus essential telephone numbers, has been left on the kitchen table. Trevor profoundly hopes the vet necessity will not arise, since the only time he tried to pick up Ozymandias he was savagely clawed in his beard.

Nevertheless, he reliably changes the cat litter, puts out Ozymandias' favourite biscuits and makes sure he has a little treat of milk. This is not good for Ozymandias, who sicks up most of it on Mrs McPhee's kelim, bought for 'very good price, madam' in a bazaar in Istanbul.

Ozymandias is also cunning about depositing dead mice in places where they can be smelled but not found. Despite this war of attrition Trevor tootles up in his tinny little car twice a day to check on Ozymandias' wellbeing, water the plants and check the McPhees' windows have been double-locked. They think he is a treasure. Ozymandias, king of kings, is never going to rise above someone who's called him cute, and wees pointedly in Joan's suitcase when she returns.

The Moth Hunt

CHRISTOPHER REALIZED AS soon as he found the hole in his cashmere jummy: it's That Time of Year Again. The clothing moth has come to haunt him – there's the little blighter up on the curtains – together with blowflies hatching in the window frames, and Muffy's found silverfish in the cutlery drawer. At first they reacted with humane repellents: Kindly Moth Death Spray, nonchemical mothballs and cedar; but the moths – isn't that one on the bookcase? – are impervious to the charms of eco-death.

When mothy inroads were made into Muffy's Jaeger wedding outfit, it was war. Christopher has emptied Peter Jones of permethrin-laden aerosols and anything oozing paradichlorobenzene. Muffy has emptied the freezer of last season's partridges and stuffed in her best clothes to permafrost any larvae. It's cheaper than dry cleaning. Television programmes are interrupted by Christopher and Muffy leaping to their feet with rolled-up newspapers to thwack a silvery pest in the pelmets. Great-Aunt Violet's Chinese vase has bitten the dust; Muffy never liked it anyway and, among the smashed bits, is very pleased to have found Granny's diamond ring she'd forgotten she hid there and has since claimed for on insurance.

Now, have they the webbing clothing moth (the most common), the casemaking clothes moth or the tapestry or carpet moth? Muffy can't fit her tatting into the deep freeze, so should they think of dry-ice fumigation, as recommended by Clothes Moths Management Guidelines?

'Are you mad, Muffy, to be thinking of bathing the house in carbon dioxide? It's all your fault, as moths prefer dirty clothes – they turn wool into food.'

Muffy is excessively irritated that Christopher is a jack-in-the-box swiping shadows, clapping fluttery moths between his hands, invoking bats, owls and bears: 'They eat moths, y'know, and I don't know why the dog can't get on a war footing. We're not talking the endangered Madagascan Sunset moth – we're talking about the savaging of my cashmere by something common.'

The Queen Bee

VIRGINIA CHUDLEIGH IS the chair of the Chilton Magna Horticultural Show, also the Chilton Bolton Choral Society, the Chilton Parva Literary Festival and the Chilton Wallop Preservation Committee. 'I find it very hard to understand people who don't give,' she booms, her muscular voice reaching one long before she does. She is dressed in the indomitable uniform of the Old Right: perm, pearls, sensible shoes and a suit with a sagging bottom. Ginny hopes that her sense of colour shows that she has a sense of humour when she hoves into meetings in her red number. Hands-on does not begin to describe her approach to the Horticultural Show, scheduled for June: they are now sitting in the church hall in January, with PG Tips and a plate of HobNobs, being harangued about their intentions towards sweet peas. 'Now, Mrs Pettigrew, you grow a fine sweet pea. How are you going to manage your cuttings? I don't want Stoke Lovage taking first prize.' Daphne Pettigrew, who thinks that she ought to be chair, bristles at being bossed but Virginia is already on to the size of Mr Featherstone's marrows – 'Keep that up, Cedric' – and the paucity of last year's egg sandwiches. 'Let no one say Chilton Magna cannot put on a spiffing tea.' Then she has gathered her briefcase, the capacious handbag, and swept out to bollock Chilton Bolton for two duffnotes in their Messiah.

All are left in her wake feeling as if they have been run over. At the Pettigrews' drinks party (Ginny now dressed in fuchsia cashmere twinnie and a black silk skirt) she buttonholes their house guest, Lord Greengrocer, about his obligation to support her literary festival. 'We're expecting Melvyn Bragg, Joanna Trollope and William Shawcross, to say the least. It is most inconsiderate of Stieg Larsson to be dead – he'd have been quite an attraction, and Chilton Parva is like Hay-on-Wye before it became so commercial.' Ollie Pettigrew observes that Graham Greengrocer is getting a twinset tirade. Virginia is unembarrassable but effective, a scary mix of *The Archers'* Linda Snell and a provincial Vivien Duffield.

The Trainspotter

TREVOR IS A gricer, not a trainspotter. He has the accoutrements of the trainspotter: notebook, pencil, Thermos, camera, soggy sandwiches, binoculars, NHS glasses held together with Sellotape, and he hangs around the end of railway platforms. But he is not a trainspotter, or even a railway enthusiast. Trevor does not want to be rebranded into modern speak, like ticket inspectors becoming revenue protection officers. He's a gricer, a railway obsessive espousing the platonic ideal that the railways represent the medieval universe, and if he can see it all the meaning of his life will be made whole.

Up with this Mrs Trevor could put only for so long. She has retreated to her sister's, saying, 'Trevor's a lovely man but knowing that the lights on the bumper beam of a 1924 Great Western are in the wrong place doesn't help with mending the washing machine.' Trevor hasn't really noticed that she's gone. His most poignant loss is that he's too young to have experienced the joys of bunking at the Toton depot in Nottingham, seeing the ten great Peak trains lined up in numerical order: Scafell Pike, Helvellyn, Skiddaw, Great Gable, Cross Fell, Whernside, Ingleborough, Penyghent, Snowdon, Tryfan. That is romance.

Hanging about at Clapham Junction (with its lovely coffee bar on platform nine) is all very well, but what Trevor wouldn't have given to have seen and noted locomotives 70005 John Milton, 70007 Coeur de Lion, 70009 Alfred the Great, 70035 Rudyard Kipling and 70040 Clive of India. The steamy clouds, the rumble of the wheels, the choo-choo-choo as the great iron horse pulled its load. The 10.58 to Woking does not have the same allure. Yet Trevor is happy: he's tipped his bobble hat to the Flying Scotsman, and is an expert on streaks, the streamlined locomotives designed by Sir Nigel Gresley – Mallard and Bittern will live in his memory for ever.

Michael Palin is a trainspotter, so it must be all right. Come the revolution, Trevor is convinced there are sixty-three Grange Class steam locomotives hidden in a siding on the east side of Box Tunnel, ready to do their duty.

The Gardening Fiends

JANET IS A nurturer, munificent with compost, blood and bone, tireless watering and the coaxing of seedlings in her potting shed. She is a champion of narcissus pseudonarcissus Lobularis, Wordsworth's small wild daffodils as he wandered lonely in the Lake District. The felicitous effects of her interplanting these with blue scillas beneath the dappled shade of the magnolia campbellii have merited visits from the Chilton Magna village garden committee. Dickie is the arbiter of arboreal doom; hard pruning is his watchword – nothing like it for conifers – the chainsaw his chosen weapon versus unruly growth and, under cover of darkness, any sycamore that dares to show its head. Little beast. 'Just trying it on, and to think they're protected. Bloody weeds.' Dickie is a devil with the strimmer, the blowing machine and the mower, never happier than when blasting through the happy peace of their Arcadian idyll with the Atco. Every egg shell is preserved so that he can grind them up in the Magimix to sprinkle round the hostas in the endless war of attrition against slugs. Tulips? Whirr-grind. Pulverized peppermints are just the thing against mice. Fortunately the little buggers only ravage tulips not daffodils. Dickie becomes so incensed by predators that he attacked the blackfly on the runner beans with washing-up liquid. Unfortunately there was a napalm effect. Janet sighed gently and said runner beans were the most frightful bore to cook anyway, and perhaps Dickie could now worry about rosemary beetles destroying the lavender. She is going to evoke an Indian summer, erecting a sunshade of cotton and bamboo, trimmed with mother-of-pearl hearts and little bells. She ordered it in a rush of blood to the head from a gardening catalogue, along with comfrey (it helps you grow marvellous organic tomatoes) and honesty, the wildflower that is a larval plant food for the orange-tip butterfly. At night in bed, inspired by their autumn break visiting the Lost Gardens of Heligan, Janet and Dickie plan a centrepiece pagoda, jungle ferns, trickling water and banana trees. Janet sleeps peacefully, dreaming about a biodiverse pond rich in frogs and dragonflies; Dickie's chainsaw nightmare is of pond sharks.

The Pollyanna

VIVIEN IS RELENTLESSLY cheerful. The recession is absolutely wonderful because we were all getting so spoilt, weren't we? Spending the rest of one's life eating sausage casserole will be such fun, and there are marvellously inventive things to be done with pigeon.

Nonetheless, Esmond saw Vivien tucking into the filet of beef with vigour. Ditto Gilly Fitzwilliam's Grand Marnier soufflé. 'So delicious, Gilly dear, you are a heroine to treat us so royally. Is there a little smidgen for seconds? I never eat pudding but this is such a wicked treat in these hard times.'

Only Vivien can reprimand with praise. The assembled company got a lecture about the virtues of Charles Dickens.

'I have just re-read *Hard Times*; we all must. Isn't it splendid that circumstances are taking us back to what really matters? I live for literature.' Everyone had an overwhelming desire to rush to the nearest Odeon to see *Confessions of a Shopaholic*.

Now, clutching her glass of reassuringly expensive Rully – 'I don't suppose there's a tiny drop more is there, Giles? You are so spoiling. Just jolly old wine box when you come to kitchen sups with little me' – she is telling Esmond how lucky he is to live alone. 'You can do what you like, when you like, and get by on a boiled egg.'

Esmond, a widower, rather liked his wife (she was a good bridge player) and stumps around the Old Manor in the time he might be doing what he likes wondering what she would have done about the Snapdragons. He can't read the daily's instructions on the frozen meals for one and there are no flowers in the drawing room any more.

Vivien is saying that she thinks loneliness is such a positive opportunity: 'A gorgeous single man like you is so sought after, you lucky boy!' Esmond is thinking that Vivien has lipstick on her teeth. Just when all could chew on a good moan, she's popped a chocolate truffle into her mouth and opined that bankers will surely give most of their pensions to charity. Esmond imagines that at Vivien's funeral they'll play 'Always Look on the Bright Side of Life'.

The Antiquarian Book Dealer

GARETH IS A solitary soul living behind a cliff of dead books. If pressed, he can tell you, with crisp authority and in the cracked and unused voice of one who doesn't speak much, that there are more words in English than in any other language. What he likes is to have them stacked in front of him, a first edition of Thackeray here, a *Jock of the Bushveld* there, perhaps Butler's *Lives of the Saints*. They are a Maginot Line of verbs, nouns, similes and rhymes against the revolting crassness of the modern world. He would prefer that nobody bought any of them, for they are his beloveds.

Anyone entering Fust and Snooze is heralded by the rusty tingting of the bell, at which point Gareth shoots his head out, like a tortoise from its shell, and challenges them to browse, buy, or even worse, to ask questions. They are impertinent trespassers in this realm of dead words, and Gareth is not prepared to ferry them across the Styx to first editions they would not deserve.

Fust and Snooze smells of foxed frontispieces, ancient leather covers and Gareth's jacket, ingrained with clubby remnants of spilled red wine. His yellow teeth click.

Given his bellicose attitude to sales, it is of no surprise that he is an expert on military history and reluctantly welcoming to colonels and generals in search of original accounts of the Battle of Waterloo. Since Gareth operates his own peculiar archive, this might be found next to A.N. Holcombe's *Public Ownership of Telephones on the Continent of Europe* or Mike Echanus' *Knife Fighting and Throwing for Combat*. Only Gareth knows.

His prize possession is a first edition of Jane Austen. It is as George IV might have read it, if George IV had ever read anything.

Prinny would probably not have been allowed in Fust and Snooze: too fat, too loud and unappreciative of the value of notes written in the margin.

To feel an original dust jacket, to touch a bookplate inscribed 'Princess Maria Obolensky', to stroke the stained leather is literary Braille to Gareth.

The Budget Traveller

JULIA KNEW IN her bones that Plummit Airlines was a mistake. The Ponsonbys were ecstatic about the joys of flying from Southampton Airport – 'So much more civilized than Heathrow' – to Bergerac, a mere hour from their converted farmhouse in Tarn et Garonne. 'Honestly, we use it like a taxi service. Simon books all the tickets online in January for about £20 each, so if we decide not to fly we just throw them away. You'll be with us in time for lunch.'

Ceci Ponsonby never mentioned that in order to achieve this idyll of foie gras and crisp, icy local wine, Julia would have to get a taxi from Badger's Court at 3.30 a.m. The aeroplane (Plummit has just the one) has now been delayed for four hours due-to-a-technical-fault-we-apologize-for-any-inconvenience. Julia is past wondering whether it's just a broken seat or the engine has fallen off.

The bacon butties at the cafe have all been scoffed by a school trip going kayaking on the Dordogne; Julia daren't get another cappuccino in case the Boris-alike at her feet upgrades himself to the seat she's bagged with pointless, time-filling purchases from duty-free. It felt surreal buying vodka and the new Donna Leon at seven o'clock. The prospect of lunch has dwindled to a tube of Pringles.

Julia's thinking furiously of her husband, comfortably in BA first class to Beijing while she is stranded among the fat, ugly people who congregate in airports these days. Surely not all with second homes in France?

They have their faces upturned like sunflowers to a departures board devoid of information. A nice, bald man is holding his head in despair and his wife has chosen the supine protest position – catatonic on the floor, a sandal occasionally twitching.

Finally aboard, they sit knee to chest. Oh joy! Bergerac airport is in sight, but who are those figures walking determinedly away? 'Ladies and gentlemen, the firemen at Bergerac have just gone on strike in sympathy with the French lorry drivers' fuel protest. We're diverting to Bordeaux.' Lunch? She'll be lucky to be chez Ponsonby for dinner. Julia resolves never to economize again.

The Rugby Player

FRED IS A tighthead prop, 6 ft 5 in and eighteen stone of brutish bigness, and plug-ugly. Not the chap to meet down a dark alley at night. Except that he is a gentle giant, has a weakness for medieval literature, and when a prefect at Dulwich College protected the fragile and gave the bullies a firm boot up the arse.

If you did meet him down a dark alley he'd be protecting a little old lady from being duffed up by a drunk. 'Now listen here, sonny, you're a disgrace to humanity.' Having picked him up by the scruff of the neck, Fred would chuck the offender into the gutter and take the little old lady home. 'Don't you worry, madam. Now have you got your keys? What you need is a nice cuppa.'

Fred's personal idea of a 'nice cuppa' is frothing beer, anointed with lavish drops of blood from the cut on his head where he was stamped on by Tosser Dorrington in the ruck. He was head of his university rugby club – 'Fred's round, chaps; he's broken another finger, but not his drinking arm' – and his wife says she can't understand why he spends every Saturday with his head up other chaps' bottoms.

'And then I have to make the tea and listen to how you pushed forward in the scrum and won rucks and mauls and drove forward with the ball. Did you know that your ears look like a pair of prize-winning cauliflowers?' Fred knows that Rosie doesn't mean it, and she makes bloody good sarnies and fruit cake.

All the Musketeers team think Rosie is a bit of all right. 'Lucky you, Fred. My Sophie just goes to Topshop all Saturday. I've broken a clavicle and she says, "How stupid is that?"'

Fred, Trev and Kev get very excited about the Six Nations. Beer is laid in. They have tickets for Twickers and every sprain, contusion, dislocation and laceration will be forgotten. Merv, Steve and Dave from the Jokers will be with them, despite having stamped on Fred and tried to gouge his eyes on the pitch. There're rules and authority, and a good handshake all round, unlike oik football. They all know all the words to 'Swing Low, Sweet Chariot'.

The Pub Quiz Team

MERVYN, BY VIRTUE of having a beard and knowing the chemical symbol for potassium, is captain of the Slam Dunkers. His wife, Sally, a librarian, is hot stuff on the Bible. She knows her Lamentations of Jeremiah, not to mention her Hosea from her Obadiah. Craig is the youth element, a treasury of football and popular culture. He was vetted by Mervyn and by George, who combines his comb-over with an abject air of disapproval, and they were mightily impressed that Craig knew the only Number One record whose title was a palindrome, performed by a group whose name was a palindrome. 'Yeah, see, like SOS. Abba.' Craig may not do joined-up speech, but he's as keen as mustard – an unfortunate colour for his shirt, given his spots.

Jethro is only there for the beer, or so he says, it being uncool for an old hippie with a ponytail to admit to competitive urges. He has unnatural knowledge of phobias, flags of the world, 1960s hit singles and the code names for airports.

BKK is as nothing to regulars of the Fat Frog, most of whom have spent unwashed hours in Bangkok airport, but what about LCT? Ah, Jethro's got you – so close to home: London City.

Gathered together on a drab Monday night, the Slam Dunkers are ready for anything the quizmaster can throw at them. 'Now, an easy one to start, ladies and gents: by what name was Baron Manfred von Richthofen better known? A) Baron Greenback. B) The Red Baron. C) Lord Flashheart. D) Biggles.' It's hardly worth Mervyn chewing his pencil.

The Slam Dunkers like a thumper: 'What is the title of the only play written by the birthcontrol pioneer Marie Stopes?' or 'Which is the most southerly and westerly racecourse in Britain?' George, a furtive punter, is on to that with Newton Abbot.

The Slam Dunkers win £25 and Jethro blows it on a round. 'Slam Dunk, mate? It's a demon American basketball shot.'

The Village Organist

ELAINE IS A treasure. Every Sunday in her little Peugeot she trundles round the churches in the amalgamated parishes now lumped together as Upton Cheviot to thump out 'Immortal, Invisible, God Only Wise'. Elaine likes proper hymns. In her view 'Lord of the Dance' has led to all sorts of unfortunate low church aberrations. She is not even very keen on 'Shine, Jesus, Shine'. If the vicar wants that sort of thing, he should get someone with a kaftan and a guitar.

The vicar doesn't want to; he is sensible enough to realize that Elaine is an essential component in retaining what congregations he has. Elaine's presence, gently playing 'God Be in My Head' at the beginning of the service, is an essential part of Sunday although, the organs being at the front of the churches, the most everyone sees of Elaine is her back, comprising yards of woolly brown skirt and drifts of woolly brown hair. Elaine likes brown, and has a collection of stern blouses to denote musical dedication. At the patronal services, Harvest Festival, Christmas, Easter and Whitsun, she makes a little corsage of a carnation and ferns to honour the seriousness of the occasion.

Elaine went to the Royal College of Music, and when she participated in a festival of organ music at the Albert Hall, the vicar took a charabanc of parishioners up to London to support her.

Elaine (in a full-length brown sateen evening dress) was very touched and the vicar felt that, however stretched the parishes' finances, it was money well spent to preserve Elaine's services. Where would the Christmas concert be without her? Elaine, during creative evenings at home with her husband (a quantity surveyor for the council) and her cat, has composed an Advent anthem.

Meanwhile, shivering congregations are watching her like hawks: when Elaine puts her mittens on to play, the church wardens finally give in and put on the heating.

The Vegetable Obsessive

BELINDA IS HAVING that Michelle Obama moment. Her vegetable plot in Little Binning may not precisely resemble the organic garden of the White House but should she ever meet the First Lady they will be able to talk green shoots. More precisely, pea shoots: rapid germination, full of vitamins. Also green lentils and green beans. 'Tell me, Michelle, do you put the water on to boil before you go out and pick your beans, and then say to the children, "These were alive twenty minutes ago," and do adorable Malia and Sasha say, "That's so gross"?' Belinda's children also vetoed white tomatoes ('Yuck! Where's the ketchup?') when she contemplated a white vegetable garden of white beetroot, white melons, white carrots, the Long White Paris cucumber and White Beauty toms, an edible Sissingshurst culled from Kitchen Garden which Belinda's husband Harry describes as vegetable porn. He's lost her at bedtime to the charms of Bob Flowerdew, with his blonde plaited hair and comforting advice that a Mediterranean climate is never going to happen here. Belinda feels that diversification into olive groves might be beyond her at this stage, despite the astonishing amount of equipment she's bought: a hoe to 'draw the line' for seedlings is Recession Woman's new handbag, a spade so much more keep-fit than pilates. Should it be seed trays or cell trays? This, she tells Harry, is the eternal question. 'What every seed needs is the built-in survival mechanism of dormancy.' Harry is an accountant – his wife could be speaking Aramaic. The chitting of potatoes, health-boosting phytochemicals in coloured veg, the hot, sick wanting feeling for a narrow windowsill propagator for aubergines are beyond mere number-crunching. When he talks about Angel Cabrera, Belinda thinks it's a type of lettuce. Angel might do really well with lollo rosso. She's debating a wigwam of sweetpeas amongst the cut-and-come-again crops like oakleaf and basil, a question for guru Sarah Raven at the Farleigh Wallop Garden & Gift Fair. Belinda wonders if Michelle finds comfort in home-grown produce now Barack's administration is in the manure.

The Party Aftermath

POLLY PROMISED HER parents it was going to be a really sweet little party: 'Just girls, y'know, Dad, like cool. I mean, we've worked dead hard this term. I just thought it'd be great, y'know, to hang out, chill in the garden. Much safer than if we went to a bar.' This was Polly's fiendishly cunning wheeze. Her father immediately imagined ten innocent fifteen-year-olds having Rohypnol slipped into Bacardi Breezers. The white slave trade and hideous scenes involving syringes in pub lavatories flashed through his mind. Polly would definitely have her party at home. Yes, he and Polly's mother promised to go out: 'Just down the road to the Gordons', so you'll know where we are.' No, they wouldn't embarrass Polly by popping in on their way back to say cooee, just go straight to bed like good parents.

Now they are confronted by a scene that makes Armageddon seem as but a Buckingham Palace garden party. Polly, in a skintight stripy top (when they'd left her in a pretty Topshop dress), buried under bodies; suspect feet sticking out of the shrubbery; and so many bottles it's going to make Polly's mother embarrassed to recycle. The strict rule was no alcohol, apart from one cocktail, parent-administered. Polly's mum had been way too enthusiastic about the party: 'So, darling, what about a fun theme? Bellinis and Blinis? Or Prosecco and Prosciutto?' Polly said whatever as long as it was pizza and Coke. 'That's Coca-Cola, Mum. And Krispy Kreme doughnuts.' Despite industrial-strength carbs, the vodka and cider Binkie Bellingham smuggled through the loo window has felled the assembled company. The parents can see a pair of discarded knickers: are there boys here? The television is still dispensing E! Entertainment, an iPod is playing a memorial loop of Michael Jackson, plus there's a cacophony of mobiles – desperate calls from other parents – cheeping down the sofa. Plant pots have sprouted digital cameras. The loos have snail-trails of sick. Some of it is stuck in the fourteen yards of hair necessary to be a credible teenager. Nobody has retained matching shoes. The parents thank God this was a private party. Too late. The pictures are already on Facebook.

The Electrician

MARK THE SPARK is doing the ritual teeth-sucking of a man faced with a furious woman about to ask him why he has put the plug halfway up the wall. 'It's the law, missus. Gotta think of the disabled.' Cherry Chuffwit thinks of few people except herself and certainly not of the infirm, who hopefully won't make it up the stairs to her boudoir. Mark, he can have a proper conversation with Chazza Chuffwit, a nice heart-to-heart about AVsystem wiring and CAT6 for the internet, but the missus is a different bag of chips. She's all recessional directional downlights. Mark's had a right nightmare with her Polestars, her Mini Starlights and her Waterlilies. 'Now, Mark, the Waterlily 50 is sealed for wet areas.' Mark recommended the Waterspring 50 LED, same idea with a 20 mm baffle to reduce glare on the old bag and 'energy efficient, missus, compliant with Part L building regs'. Cherry is not having it, surmising that energy efficiency is a government conspiracy to interfere with the tasteful design of her beautiful home. 'The Waterlily matches the Polestars, Mark, so that is what I am going to have. You can put those hideous energy-thing bulbs in the home cinema and the utility room, then remove them the moment the building inspector has gone.' More teeth-sucking. Now these 'ere plugs ... you know wot? It has to be silver-nickel plates. Bit of bling. She'll love 'em. Then he can have a soothing confab with Chazza about wireless lighting controls and the Grafik Eye 3000 series. 'It's like this, Gov: it's your multi-scene preset lighting control system, from a single feed. Ideal for your open-plan living space. Flick-of-a-switch stuff – trust me, it's the dog's bananas. There's your auxiliary control with personalized light-up engravings. See this 'ere? It has press buttons for home, away, entertain – the missus'll be doing a lot of that, I'll be bound – and goodnight.' Game over, Chazza's a pushover for a bit of tech. Back to the missus for track lighting in the kitchen. 'I'm not spending £50,000 on Bulthaup and no one seeing it spot-lit. And I want lightstream under the cookery books.' Mark wants his tea.

The Englishman Abroad

EDMUND DOES NOT like the sun – particularly foreign sun with its attendant demons of suncream, sunglasses and sunny dispositions. While he is slathering the few visible parts of himself in anti-sun and anti-mosi, others are exposing injudicious bits of themselves in the swimming pool, giggling away, unaware of the carcinogenic properties of sunshine.

Edmund feels sad for them, and has a suck of his pink gin under the umbrella tree where he's reading Herodotus while making sure that his long-sleeve shirt covers his wrists.

The sun shall not shine on anywhere; nor the mosquito be tempted by delicate white flesh. He wore his panama as he was leaving Hampshire; better not to trust things to chance. This instantly identified him as the Man Who Would Not be Able to Cope with Self-Check-in. Buxom BA gels came and helped him; 'Caribbean, sir? Lucky you.' He preferred to call it the West Indies. His wife, Felicity, had said, 'Shooting's over in Feb, old thing. I've been cooking brown food for months for your mates. Let's go and stay with the Andrews; old family house, Italianate garden, and the cook is perfectly frightful so you'll feel entirely at home. So chop, chop and do the decent thing.'

Got to keep the dear girl happy; the female of the species likes a bit of sun. Nothing a Sundowner won't sort. Edmund was bemused to be told that house rules included not wearing shoes; so he's stuck firmly to his socks. You may take the chap out of Winchester, but you can't take Winchester out of the chap. Sand? Bloody awful, gritty stuff. You don't want to have anything to do with it. Sea? Turbulent, untrustworthy; beware locals vroom-vrooming on jetskis. Sun? Frightful yellow thing, horribly hot. Edmund scuttles from shade to shade with piping inquiries about whether, in the cool of the evening, it might be possible to visit Noël Coward's old house.

The Trainer's Wife

ANNABEL IS SO sparky. Her alarm clock for her unpaid job goes off at 5.45 a.m., at which point she boots her hung-over husband out of bed to head for the gallops.

'Shave, Harry, for God's sake. Sheikh Ali's manager is coming down to look at Archangel.' Sometimes she rides out herself, elfin in stretchy cream jodhpurs, and then is back to cook the full English for owners just pitching up. 'Oh, er, Annabel, coffee? Thanks. Where's Harry? Rather thought I'd go and see Crackerjack put through his paces. Hmm, can I take a sausage in my fingers, darling?'

Annabel's drinks tray is braced at all times. Ditto her kettle. 'Coffee? Tea? Whisky? Honestly, no probs.' She has a Bloody Mary mixed – 'I say, Annabel, you are the absolute bestest' – ready for the off on Sunday mornings when everyone chews the fat.

Obviously it was a bummer that Black Mamba, was pipped in the 3.45 at Chepstow. The stable's darling, Mamby, is a bit pamby and all his twenty owners want to know the reason why.

That's the trouble with these huge syndicates: each owner feels entitled to discuss the horse with Harry at length, making him even more taciturn, and the predations on the drinks tray are terrible. Annabel, while gently kicking a dog off the sofa with a velvet slipper, thinks expenditure on alcohol even outstrips the vet's bills.

When they have a runner Annabel scrubs up in her coat and hat, and tries to remember to take off her gumboots to drive Harry to the racecourse while he studies the form. Once there she's smiling and terribly nice to everyone, admirable considering she can't drink because of chauffeuring Harry back to Lambourn for an evening of reruns on the racing channel. Sometimes Annabel wonders if there is anything else on television, any newspaper other than the *Racing Post* or anyone who isn't having an affair. Keeping track of the multiple marriages within the racing fraternity is almost as tiring as the smiling. And always having to get out of bed while it is still dark.

The Lawn Fetishist

GARRY IS OUT with his Green Reaper premium power force mower at the first intimation of regeneration. God forbid the grass should actually be allowed to grow after the hours he has spent on scarification, aeration, nutrition and fertilization. There is nothing Garry cannot tell you, and does, about the evils of grass thatch and the humid moist conditions that conspire to nurture fungal lawn predators. Red thread and fairy rings evoke savage feelings within his breast. Moles! Heaven help the mole that ever dared to surface on Garry's verdant sward.

Mrs Garry is not allowed to have a dog because of the perils of urination. Brown patches would excoriate Garry's sensibilities. Next door the neighbours loll in an arboreal mess, their lawn a tangle of charming daisies and dandelions, leaves on the bough shading pre-priandial dalliance with an icy bottle of Pinot Grigio. Not that they can actually hear themselves speak as Garry mows in perfect stripes next door. Leaves! The shade would impair lawn growth, possibly creating the need for overseeding. Garry has lopped off the branches on his side of the fence; flowers are only allowed to grow in pots, or annuals planted out exactly eight inches apart. Vroom! Vroom! Garry's mower's turbostar system for unparalleled airflow is hitting top gear. The neighbours are on the second bottle, mouthing about how much they love the smell of new mown grass. Fortunately Garry has learnt from *Gardeners' World* that mowing less frequently reduces stress to the grass; mow too low and there is the hideous possibility of scalping. Garry is obsessive about his blades; blunt or dull blades could shred the tops of the grass leaves and expose tissue to diseases. No hospital matron is more chary of MRSA than Garry is of lawn pests. Chafer grubs, the larvae of the crane fly, the Daddy-Long-Legs and leatherjackets could lead to total loss of the lawn. Just as it's reached velvet green status, and Garry can rejoice in the lack of worm casts, Mrs Garry says what with the lawn being so luverly she's asked friends round for a barbecue. What? People are not meant to actually stand on it.

The Stately Galleon

AUGUSTA SAILS INTO a room with the confidence of one wearing vintage Balenciaga and a fearsome manicure. She wafts upon a cloud of Arpege; her jewellery probably accounts for most of the mislaid Amber Room. Behind her, deep in the environs of a small coat cupboard, a maid is indubitably staggering under the weight of hanging Augusta's mink coat.

As this vision bears down upon a large whisky, no-one could possibly confuse it with a bulbous mass of lard. Augusta is the living contradiction of size zero; Augusta is an icon, the Boadicea of the art world. Augusta knew Gilbert and George before Gilbert knew George. Augusta espoused Chris Ofili and his elephant dung. Where art historian Mildred Dreeb saw pornography, Augusta saw references to William Blake 'And darlings, there's glitter in the elephant dung that is psychodynamically witty.' Thus she makes women the width of a single strand of spaghetti look intellectually starved. On anyone else a halter neck dress might appear to be an over the shoulder boulder holder; on Augusta it is a Viking prow. Her embonpoint promises largesse, excess, abundance. She is known as a marvellous cook, her refrigerator a preservation zone for double cream and Normandy butter. Augusta sautés fresh foie gras with port – 'Much less drying than brandy' – and tosses linguine with said cream and caviar. 'Then really all one needs is a green salad.' Gathered around her table may be poets, Armenian art dealers and competitors for the Tangerine Prize for women's fiction. She also has a tendresse for mothy aristocrats because one never knows when they may need to sell a Gainsborough. Augusta wouldn't be Augusta if she didn't have a hotline to Christoby's or know the sort of perfectly charming Americans who want their houses on Park Avenue to look like the Frick Museum. The perfectly charming Americans are terrified Augusta won't fit in their elevators. Since their body mass index is threatened by a lettuce leaf, they are also confused by her projectile superiority. Have they been so busy detoxing that fat's become fashionable?

The War Baby

LUCIA'S TIME HAS come: again. Having appreciated the fruits of digging for victory and nurtured her mother's hens through rationing – there was always a proper omelette at the Harrington-Whiteleys, no powdered egg muck – Lucia is again a domestic goddess. Her son, who laughed at the autumn obsession with windfall apples and chutney and Ma recycling Sunday's leg of lamb into shepherd's pie, is now accusing his wife of reckless extravagance every time an M&S ready meal darkens their PoggleBaulp designer kitchen. 'Do you know how much that cost? We've got to cut these food bills. My mother could make a leg of lamb last until Wednesday.'

This is not what Honeysuckle, born into the Which-Restaurant-Tonight generation, wants to hear. Honeysuckle doesn't do mince. She never thought her mother-in-law's plum-bottling skills were anything other than something old people did. Now they're being held against her as the miracle cure for the credit crunch.

Unaware of the shopping bill Gestapo, Lucia serenely plucks blackberries from the Dorset hedgerows. Earlier in the year she gathered elderflowers to make cordial and sloes for sloe gin. Nothing like free food from nature's bounty. The start of the shooting season will produce sad little partridge carcases, deliciously roasted at a dinner party with Lucia's homegrown potatoes and red cabbage, then boiled into oblivion for stock. Nothing is wasted. What the sweet chickens don't get, the compost heap does. A nice bit of mould on the homemade marmalade is pure penicillin; sell-by dates are just common.

Lucia was eco long before the Greens adopted hessian shopping bags. 'Eco is a buzzword,' says Honeysuckle, who is in marketing. 'Really, dear? Could you pass me those prawn shells? I'm going to make bisque.' Grandchildren are sent outside to whisk egg whites in copper bowls with fresh air – vital – for meringues, while the yolks are being made into hollandaise for Grandpa's trout.

Last year's pheasants exhumed from the freezer will be eaten up à la normande, with cream swapped with Mrs Bagshaw for chutney. They're going to get through the lean times with largesse.